Reforming International Extradition

Reforming International Extradition

Fairness, Individual Rights and Justice

Sally Kennedy and Ian Warren

ANTHEM PRESS

Anthem Press
An imprint of Wimbledon Publishing Company
www.anthempress.com

This edition first published in UK and USA 2024
by ANTHEM PRESS
75–76 Blackfriars Road, London SE1 8HA, UK
or PO Box 9779, London SW19 7ZG, UK
and
244 Madison Ave #116, New York, NY 10016, USA

British Library Cataloguing-in-Publication Data
A catalogue record for this book is available from the British Library.

Library of Congress Cataloging-in-Publication Data
A catalog record for this book has been requested.
2024932714

ISBN-13: 978-1-83998-957-5 (Pbk)
ISBN-10: 1-83998-957-2 (Pbk)

This title is also available as an e-book.

CONTENTS

ABBREVIATIONS

Canadian Charter	*Canadian Charter of Rights and Freedoms* 1982
CAT	*Convention against Torture and Other Cruel, Inhuman or Degrading Treatment or Punishment* 1984
Budapest Convention	*Convention on Cybercrime* 2001
Refugee Convention	*Convention Relating to the Status of Refugees* 1951
ICCPR	*International Covenant on Civil and Political Rights* 1966
EAW	European Arrest Warrant
ECHR	*European Convention on Human Rights* 1950
ECtHR	European Court of Human Rights
EU	European Union
NZ	New Zealand
TCC	Transnational Criminal Court
UK	United Kingdom
UN	United Nations
US	United States
UDHR	*Universal Declaration of Human Rights* 1948

Introduction

EXTRADITION AND TRANSNATIONAL JUSTICE

Introduction

Extradition treaties and related domestic legislation regulate the lawful transfer of individuals accused or convicted of criminal offences to the prosecuting jurisdiction (Bassiouni 2008; Cullen and Burgess 2015; Griffith and Harris 2005). While the physical surrender may be technically lawful under these mechanisms, there are many circumstances which raise concerns about the fairness of extradition. A lawful surrender often creates the appearance that any subsequent prosecution, conviction and sentence is fair or just. Many extradition cases address claims associated with individual rights, which can include widely accepted international human rights protections, domestic due process principles and broader individual rights. All these issues are discussed in the case studies presented in this book.

Extradition is regulated by layers of bi- or multilateral treaties (Magnuson 2012), as well as quasi-criminal domestic legislation and in some cases constitutional requirements, such as in the United States (US) (Bassiouni 2008; Nadelmann 1990). As 'domestic legal arrangements are predicated on international legal arrangements' (Cullen and Burgess 2015, 236), international extradition is a highly unusual area of law. At its core, extradition involves the prosecution of 'national crimes subject to transnational criminal procedure' to ensure the individual appears in court to exercise their right to defend charges or serve a previously imposed sentence (Boister 2015, 20). Importantly, there is no 'positive obligation' on any country to extradite under international law (United Nations Office on Drugs and Crime 2012, para. 92). Extradition is also portrayed as an important form of extraterritorial power (Blakesley 1984) that reflects legal pluralism (Berman 2005; Boister 2015; Merry 1988).

Historically, extradition mainly applied to a fugitive accused of a crime in one jurisdiction who fled to another to escape prosecution or a legally imposed punishment. However, due to contemporary patterns of globalisation and technological developments such as the internet, extradition requests can now involve extraditees who, at the time of the crime, were never physically located in the nation seeking to prosecute (Allely et al. 2022; Mann et al. 2018). As nations are increasingly concerned about controlling both domestic and transnational crimes that might affect their national security (Aas 2011a, 2011b; Andreas and Nadelmann 2006; Bowling 2011; Zedner 2010), extradition becomes a reflection of international comity and strong bi- and multilateral political relationships (Abelson 2009; Bassiouni 2003; Blakesley 1984; Magnuson 2012; Sheptycki 2011). This is because the transfer of extraditees is considered to reflect compliance with relevant crime control treaties (Guzman 2002, 2005; Magnuson 2012). Increasing global interconnectedness, international travel and potentially porous national borders (Abbell 2010; Raustiala 2009) have resulted in increased consideration of extradition as a core method of promoting transnational and international justice, in a context where most investigations and prosecutions are undertaken via domestic criminal justice processes (Warren and Palmer 2015).

Statistics from Australia suggest that requests for extradition are increasing. For example, between 2005 and 2006, Australia made 13 new extradition requests and received 21 from other countries (Attorney-General's Department 2006). These rates increased from 2010 to 2011, when Australia made 22 new requests and received 23 extradition applications (Attorney-General's Department 2011). When compared to the previous period, the number of requests made by Australia decreased to six in 2015 to 2016, while the number of requests received increased to 28 (Attorney-General's Department 2016). For the 2021–2022 reporting period, the Attorney-General's Department (2022) illustrates that Australia sent 11 applications and received 35 requests. Although these statistics do not provide information about where these 35 requests come from, during the 2021–2022 period Australia surrendered two individuals to the US and the United Kingdom (UK), one person to Romania and another to the Republic of Korea. The extraditees were surrendered for offences involving fraud, driving occasioning injury, money laundering, cyber offences and sexual assault.

Statistical data from other nations is not easily accessible. For example, Edmonds-Poli and Shirk (2018) highlighted the difficulty in obtaining current and accurate data on extradition involving the US, as many cases concern sensitive law enforcement procedures and different government departments are subject to varying reporting requirements. Evidence from the US Marshals Service indicated the number of cases of surrender between 2003 and 2016 declined slightly from approximately 600 in 2008 and 2009 to below 400 in 2015 and 2016. The closest geographic neighbours to the US are also its most common extradition partners, with an average of one in ten US extradition cases during this period involving Mexico, while Canada issued and received most of its extradition requests to and from the US (Corbett 2002).

Rose (2002) has argued that some scholars believe extradition is fulfilling its main aim of transferring individuals to the prosecuting nation. This conclusion reflects a contract theory of extradition, with 'the two states being the parties, the delivery of the criminal the subject matter, and the repression of crime, undertaken by the demanding state, the consideration' (Moore 1891, 4). The contract theory is a legacy of the historical approach to extradition, which prioritises the interests of the two states under relevant extradition treaties, while placing trust in domestic criminal proceedings to uphold appropriate standards of due process and procedural fairness to protect the suspect.

However, throughout the twentieth and twenty-first centuries, it has become increasingly apparent that the prospect of extradition can unreasonably affect the individual rights or welfare of a suspect wanted for prosecution in a requesting jurisdiction (Mann et al. 2018). This places a significant responsibility on national courts when deciding whether to honour a foreign extradition request, as the individual rights and welfare of the extraditee must be considered alongside the obligations under the extradition treaty (Dugard and Van den Wyngaert 1998; Griffith and Harris 2005). For example, even when an extradition treaty aims to promote closer bilateral legal relations, some jurisdictions have routinely exempted the extradition of their nationals. This is because it is believed they are 'likely to receive ill treatment or an unfair trial in the requesting state' (Plachta 1999, 87).

In critically analysing these processes through six prominent cases decided in various English-speaking jurisdictions, this book argues that the established mechanism for extradition is no longer suited to the interests of twenty-first century transnational justice. It is becoming clear that 'a global framework [is needed for] transnational forms of crime and criminal justice' (Friedrichs 2007, 6) given persistent questions over the 'appropriateness of conventional legal paradigms' for dealing with extradition (Bowling and Sheptycki 2015, 170). Established methods for transnational criminal procedure and justice administration generate considerable tensions between domestic and international laws, the actual or optimum roles of judicial and executive decision-making, as well as the desire to promote international political relations and the rights of individual extraditees. These tensions cannot easily be reconciled and the key 'challenge facing extradition law is to reasonably accommodate the conflicting interests at play' (Arnell 2018, 869). While eliminating extradition completely could lead to problematic alternatives, such as abduction by agents of the requesting nation, informal surrender without a legal process or the use of immigration laws to deport foreign nationals subject to an extradition request (Rebane 1995, 1656), several scholars have noted valid options for adjusting existing approaches to this form of transnational justice administration. This book will explore some of these potential reforms, while emphasising the importance of defendant-centred approaches which focus on protecting individual human and due process rights (Gless 2013, 2015).

This introductory chapter outlines the operation of the extradition process which, in most cases, involves a series of executive decisions and related judicial proceedings and appeals. Other influencing factors, such as the centrality of promoting international political relations and the limits of current criminological theory, are also discussed. The continued relevance and impact of territorial sovereignty on both the criminal justice process and extradition as a quasi-criminal and quasi-administrative procedure is then illustrated, alongside some of the normative assumptions that inform extradition law. These assumptions, many of which are enshrined in dated legal principles, can cause problems when attempting to reconcile individual rights and protections with the processes of ensuring legal cooperation between nation states. This is followed by a discussion of the reasoning behind the six cases selected for analysis and a brief outline of the content of each chapter.

The Extradition Process

An extraditee has a right to voluntarily surrender to face a trial or sentence in a nation that issues an extradition request or can legally challenge the process in the domestic courts of the jurisdiction where they are located. When an extraditee decides to legally challenge a surrender request, common law nations invoke similar procedures that aim to enact the requirements specified in a bi- or multilateral extradition treaty. National legislation in each jurisdiction contains minor differences regarding the availability of bail, evidence requirements and limited rights of appeal (Abbell 2010; Aughterson 2005; Blakesley 1980).

A person's extraditability is determined through a combination of judicial and executive decisions once a request is received. First, the relevant justice authorities in the receiving state will screen the extradition request to determine if it conforms to requirements specified under the relevant treaty, and if so, issue a warrant to arrest the extraditee. Second, the extraditee can elect to voluntarily surrender or challenge the request in a domestic court. This involves the courts in the requested nation interpreting and applying the terms of the request in light of the requirements of the relevant extradition treaty and domestic legislation (Iraola 2009). An extradition hearing bears 'a striking functional resemblance to a trial' with fewer due process protections (Bifani 1993, 657) and is perhaps more akin to a pretrial hearing to determine whether a domestic criminal case should proceed to a full trial. Extradition will generally be certified if there is sufficient evidence to justify prosecution in the requested country had the conduct occurred there (Abbell 2010; Bassiouni 2008). This means factual guilt or innocence is not strictly considered during extradition proceedings. If the judiciary determines a person is extraditable, the executive branch of government considers broader political and humanitarian concerns prior to ordering an extraditee's surrender (Bassiouni 2008). This includes seeking any assurances from the requesting nation relating to protection or post-extradition concerns raised by the extraditee, including any requirements necessary to protect their fundamental human rights.

Each judicial challenge to an extradition request involves consideration of legal and political factors which can be highly technical and complex. The result is that extradition represents a:

> *mixed* proceeding. It is uneasily caught between classification as a criminal and non-criminal trial, it is uneasily caught between the judicial and executive branches, and its objects are uneasily caught, as potential claimants of legal protections, between aliens and citizens. (Bifani 1993, 693, emphasis in original)

Various factors associated with transnational legal cooperation mean that the application of international treaties in domestic courts is often revised 'in an endless loop of interpretation' (Andreas and Nadelmann 2006; Warren and Palmer 2015; Wong 1998, 111). Anderson (1983, 153) has argued 'international relations have dominated extradition law and practice', while 'notions about international good faith' often shape domestic legislation and individual extradition rulings (Miller 2016, 185). This can potentially undermine the idea of legal neutrality in extradition cases (Magnuson 2012). The influence of political factors often means extradition becomes a 'rubber-stamp judicial procedure' for governments with strong colonial, cultural or linguistic ties (Bassiouni 2003, 401). Rather than ensuring procedural fairness for prospective extraditees, the end result of existing procedures has created 'confusing extradition jurisprudence' (Gregg 2002, 125), that is characterised by unpredictable outcomes within and across jurisdictions (Arnell 2013; Cullen and Burgess 2015; Miller 2009) and greater executive streamlining to enhance efficiency. Administrative streamlining is also evident to offset some of the limits of existing legal approaches. This can be seen with the European Arrest Warrant (EAW) which is a simplified cross-border procedure to transfer individuals between Member States of the European Union (EU) (Warren and Palmer 2015).

Treaty Compliance and Criminological Theories

Adding to the complexity of the process is that most theories of extradition are reverse engineered from individual cases. This means underlying theories of extradition are drawn from complex rules and practices that vary considerably between nations. This helps to explain why judicial challenges to extradition are often highly technical, confusing, time-consuming and expensive. Coherent transnational policies and theories connecting international extradition agreements with national actions are also lacking (Guzman 2002, 1826). As transnational criminal justice systems remain undeveloped, an artificial line exists between the practice of national courts on the 'inside' and the international 'outside' that encompasses the desire to uphold bi- and multilateral political comity (Häkli 2013). Moreover, conventional criminological theories cannot fully explain cases that simultaneously involve multiple countries and justice systems (Loader and Percy 2012) and provide limited insight into the reasons behind extradition decisions, or how broader criminological concepts might impact specific cases.

For example, treaty development and compliance theories, such as the transnational legal process theory developed by Koh (1996), indicate that state and non-state actors will interact and create patterns of behaviour to serve their own short- or long-term political interests. These objectives are then incorporated into domestic legislation, which can lead to compliance in future interactions. As external behaviour is internalised, repeated action solidifies and promotes a country's national identity within the international environment. Therefore, the extent to which a jurisdiction develops domestic extradition legislation, and the ability of the judiciary and executive to interpret and enforce relevant principles, will arguably indicate its willingness to comply with a treaty (Magnuson 2012).

Additionally, a rational choice approach established by Goldsmith and Posner (1999, 2003) suggests domestic legislation enhances a nation's compliance with international law by increasing the strength of the agreement and any related sense of obligation to comply with its terms. The expectation to comply is generally made clear by signing the treaty and nations are aware that short-term cooperation is likely to lead to long-term mutual gains. This means treaties are unlikely to be violated because nations fear retaliation and the loss of their international reputation that can affect future cooperation.

Guzman's (2002, 2005) compliance-based theory brings together the ideas of Koh (1996) and Goldsmith and Posner (1999, 2003). Drawing on international relations theory, this approach describes states as self-interested actors that negotiate and comply with agreements to facilitate cooperation and increase their credibility on the international stage by avoiding direct or reputational sanctions. As the stakes increase and the issues addressed become more important, such as protecting national security, the ability of international reputation to shape a nation's compliance with a treaty reduces. Overall, countries will be hesitant to compromise positive reputations because strengthening their long-term relationships with treaty partners will be considered more important. However, if a country's international reputation is already poor or the benefits of non-compliance appear to outweigh the loss of reputation, a treaty violation is more likely.

Despite the compelling nature of these theories, knowledge about why nations choose to follow or violate an extradition agreement remains scarce. While viewed as a 'product of rational interchanges between states' to develop a form of transnational justice, the enforcement of extradition arrangements simultaneously respects each nation's pre-existing sovereign power (Magnuson 2012, 843). Therefore, nations create extradition agreements because they want to facilitate cooperation and comply because of a 'normative obligation' to uphold the treaty on their own terms (Goldsmith and Posner 2003, 141). However, Guzman (2002, 2005) questions why treaties are required when international law also regulates many aspects of transnational conduct. Consequently, current compliance theories fail to completely explain how international cooperation and domestic legal processes impact extradition (Brewster 2004). Magnuson (2012, 897) has suggested this can create 'compliance uncertainty', because it is not clear what actions will equate with conformity given there is no independent or jurisdictionally neutral process that can determine whether an extradition decision has followed treaty requirements. Therefore, the doubt surrounding what non-compliance entails can be used by nations to argue that an extradition decision may not technically be a treaty violation.

There is also no single transnational criminological theory that encompasses the domestic legislative, executive and judicial elements of extradition (Forst 2001). The lack of a comprehensive transnational justice theory means criminology's 'centre of gravity' remains focused primarily on Western countries (Aas 2012, 6). This emphasis often fails to accommodate diverse approaches to issues of common international concern (Connell and Dados 2014; Stamatel 2009). It also means that idiosyncratic or inappropriate criminal policy reforms established by powerful nations can be readily exported as normative or desired standards for the rest of the world to aspire to and follow (Chan 2000). Therefore, developing societies are often forced to integrate established international and transnational justice theories, rather than advance new models that truly enhance horizontal collaboration (Aas 2011b; Boister 2012; Carrington et al. 2016). This includes the 'internationalization of crime control' methods adopted by

Western powers that 'export their domestically derived definitions of crime' (Andreas and Nadelmann 2006, vii). This tendency creates 'context-free responses to global challenges' that become normalised as core international standards (Aas 2012, 11). Consequently, many criminological theories and concepts, including those related to extradition, focus on the specific problems affecting Western countries. This leaves criminology 'culture-bound and culture-blind', rather than addressing common international and transnational justice issues in a genuinely cooperative manner (Karstedt 2001, 295).

These factors require a willingness to understand the legal theories and practices of other nations (Blakesley and Lagodny 1991) and the 'complexities of the global' (Aas 2007, 296). However, critical legal and criminological theories have been slow to identify and address concerns associated with extradition as an established form of transnational justice cooperation (Andreas and Nadelmann 2006; Magnuson 2012). This has occurred despite a growing commitment among all nations to identify and respond to various forms of transnational and international crime (Marmo and Chazal 2016; Natarajan 2019). Given the lack of coherent transnational theories or policies that appropriately connect international extradition agreements with national actions (Guzman 2002, 1826), a series of extremely disjointed rules, procedures and practices characterises the operation of this important branch of law.

Territorial Sovereignty

As many branches of law, including the criminal law, have '"spilled out" beyond the borders of the nation-state' (Cotterrell 2012, 500), the status of extradition as a quasi-criminal form of jurisprudence has become apparent. Globalisation 'changes the meaning of place and the location and significance of boundaries' that are tied to all facets of criminal justice administration (Nelken 2011, 190), which spans the power of police to investigate crime, the capacity of courts to adjudicate questions of law and procedure and the power to punish. The global stretching of legal boundaries generates a paradox between forces that promote the increased transnational movement of people and goods, and territorial sovereignty which confines criminal jurisdiction to established state, provincial and national borders (Warren and Palmer 2015).

While cross-border offending can simultaneously activate the domestic legislation of multiple nations, which can result in competition for legal and enforcement authority (Berman 2005; Blakesley 1984; Buxbaum 2009; Dorsett and McVeigh 2012), the physical border as a marker for territorial sovereignty remains an 'incredibly potent force' that places geographic limits on the power of all criminal justice agents (Miller 2009, 650). Territorial sovereignty also validates extradition arrangements that provide a form of extraterritorial justice authority made possible through the negotiation of bi- or multilateral treaties (Epps 2003, 372) that only remains enforceable through domestic legal and justice procedures. Therefore, extradition is a partial exception to the rules of territorial sovereignty that commonly limit criminal jurisdiction to behaviour that occurs solely within a nation's borders. This is because the suspect's alleged conduct in generating the act from another location or fleeing a jurisdiction where the criminal act has allegedly occurred activates the need for a series of requests to, or permissions from, the nation where they are located to secure their apprehension and surrender.

Geographic mobility means that territorial sovereignty is an increasingly 'complex and much contested notion' within established criminal legal systems (Garland 1996, 448). However, the geographic location of criminal conduct remains the driving force behind determinations of criminal authority in English-speaking common law countries and, in turn, underpins all extradition requests and decisions (Abbell 2010, 77). This is despite requests acting as a form of extraterritorial authority generated by the requesting state. In fact, extradition can exploit the restrictions of territorial sovereignty by manipulating transnational justice processes to suit a particular legal or political end (Bowling and Sheptycki 2015). The insistence that transnational criminal laws be enforced exclusively through existing domestic legal processes invariably hampers the development of novel forms of justice cooperation that could emerge in an increasingly 'interconnected world' to address shared transnational or global legal problems (Berman 2005, 529). This is because existing criminal laws, justice procedures and the criminological frameworks that inform them remain 'trapped in a language of sovereignty with its purportedly clear lines of demarcation, its assumed allocation of authority, and its formalistic conventions of legitimacy' (Berman 2012, 337). Without an 'integrated world system' (Aas 2007, 297), territorial sovereignty has persisted as the dominant concept for any nation to 'promulgate, adjudicate and enforce its laws' (Blakesley 2008, 97). This contributes to the continued underdevelopment of both transnational and international criminal law (Blakesley 1982; Stamatel 2009; Zumbansen 2010). As a key form of transnational governance, extradition is legally subject to and politically 'obsessed with sovereignty' (Valverde 2009, 145) because it relies on established national and subnational criminal justice processes that are 'stubbornly circumscribed by geographic limits' (Blakesley 1981, 2008; Urbas 2012, 1).

The paradox between the increasingly global nature of some criminal conduct that is only enforceable at national and subnational levels rests at the heart of many concerns over the viability and fairness of current extradition procedures. As this book demonstrates, the problems raised in many contemporary cases involving international extradition reflect the disjuncture between the increased social demands for more rigorous transnational investigative procedures and the reliance on domestic laws to ensure appropriate enforcement and legal protection for potential extraditees.

Normative Assumptions behind Extradition

Extradition is underpinned by a range of legal concepts that aim to protect the integrity of the criminal justice systems of requesting and requested nations, rather than the specific rights and interests of the extraditee (Colquhoun 2000; Warren and Palmer 2015). This results from a series of outdated normative assumptions about the role of extradition which have questionable relevance in the current global environment (see Botting 2005). These assumptions include the following:

- Extradition is a requirement for the administration of transnational justice.
- A crime has been committed that warrants formal investigation or prosecution in the requesting state.
- The extraditee is a fugitive.
- The requesting nation has a right to charge and bring the extraditee to trial or to serve a sentence.
- The requested nation has an obligation to transfer the extraditee.
- The extraditee can legally challenge extradition and potentially be protected from surrender.
- Variations in the rules between common and civil law traditions are consistent and acceptable.
- Judicial and executive discretion is used sparingly.
- Each theory underpinning extradition has a discernible influence on how a specific case is approached by justice authorities.
- Extradition conforms with human rights requirements aimed at protecting the extraditee.

These normative assumptions fail to address important practical questions about the relevance or application of international human rights protections or varied domestic legal conceptions of due process. For example, the rule of non-inquiry refers to the practice where extradition courts routinely refuse to investigate the justice procedures of requesting countries. Put another way, issues relating to the potential fairness of the case must be decided based on local standards (*Adamas* 2013, para. 402), rather than through an interrogation of the methods of justice administration adopted in the nation making the request. Along with modified or restrictive evidentiary requirements, judicial deference to the executive and the limited responsibilities of the requested nation to protect the extraditee from potential harm after surrender, these legal technicalities have significant potential to reinforce the normative assumptions that have informed extradition throughout history, by limiting consideration of viable human rights claims that have emerged in more recent times (Arnell 2013; Harrington 2005; Piragoff and Kran 1992). This is because these normative assumptions ultimately serve to subordinate 'individual rights to policy interests' (Bifani 1993, 630), while at the same time prioritising state rights in the quest for enhanced transnational and international criminal justice cooperation.

The paradox that has emerged between globalisation and territorial sovereignty provides the appropriate frame of reference for questioning the normative assumptions underpinning contemporary extradition theories and practices. In this respect, this book's objective is to use the case studies presented in Chapters 2 and 3 as a basis for questioning the underlying legal and procedural rationales for extradition at a time when many alternative possibilities for achieving more just or fairer outcomes can be developed.

Case Selection

The six cases analysed in this book were carefully selected to highlight a mix of key factual details, such as the nations involved, offence type, current case status and prominent individual rights issues. While these cases ultimately determined an extraditee's eligibility for surrender, each raised several arguments against transfer central to understanding the tensions between globalisation and territorial sovereignty that underpin this area of quasi-criminal law. This book cannot possibly cover all of these issues. Instead, each case will be discussed in relation to a primary rights-based issue and a secondary concern which demonstrates broader problems with the extradition procedure, while emphasising the role of extradition courts in understanding and protecting an individual's fundamental rights.

The six cases are presented in two chapters based on the primary rights-based issue that emerges in each reported legal ruling. The first group of cases focuses on specific concerns about the physical or mental welfare of the extraditees. This includes concerns about the extraditee's mental health and associated risk of suicide (Julian Assange), allegations of persecution and torture the extraditee is likely to face if surrendered (Dorin Savu) and potential violations of the *Convention against Torture and Other Cruel, Inhuman or*

Degrading Treatment or Punishment (CAT) (1984) in the requesting jurisdiction (Elias Perez).

The three cases examined in Chapter 3 frame the rights-based issue in terms of the specific conduct of the requesting or requested nations when issuing or responding to an extradition request. This includes a case questioning the legality of a police raid, search and seizure of evidence in the requested country (Kim Dotcom), the reliability and admissibility of evidence to support a case for surrender or ensuing prosecution in the requesting state (Hassan Diab) and issues associated with the legality of formal communications between nations associated with an extradition request (Daniel Snedden).

Each case study also reveals a range of secondary issues that emerge from the extradition process. These include the extensive delays associated with some extradition requests (Julian Assange), the extraditee's status as a refugee (Dorin Savu), the practical operation of the rule of non-inquiry (Elias Perez), the process for determining double criminality (Kim Dotcom), the result of a continued campaign by the requesting nation to seek the extraditee's surrender (Hassan Diab) and the role of the political offence exception in the context of international crime (Daniel Snedden). These issues are intricately linked to the relevance and impact of individual protections considered by extradition courts when a request is received. Overall, the case selection and issues emphasised illustrate how extradition proceedings grapple with the rights of individuals in light of the priorities of the states involved as executors of extradition treaties, and how the ensuing tensions between these competing rights are reconciled by domestic courts. Table 1 provides a summary of key elements of the six cases that are explored in greater depth in Chapters 2 and 3.

Each case description in Chapters 2 and 3 provides a chronological summary of relevant factual issues, including the allegations informing the extradition request, and a summary of each primary and secondary legal issue considered by the courts of the state receiving the request. Often, these issues are highly technical. Throughout, this book seeks to educate readers on relevant factual and legal issues that emerged in each case, while addressing the underlying rationales for the decisions in light of the theoretical and practical tensions that affect extradition law.

In describing the complexity of issues emerging in these six cases, the overall objective is to provide insight into this complex area of quasi-criminal law that is of growing importance as concerns relating to globalisation extend to the fields of applied criminology and criminal justice. It is hoped these processes can become more amenable to reconciling the tensions between individual and state rights, which rests at the foundation of the need for the reform to contemporary extradition law.

Table 1 Summary of cases

Extraditee	Nations Involved	Offence	Primary Issue and Outcome	Secondary Issue and Outcome
Welfare of extraditees				
Julian Assange	*Request 1* Requesting: Sweden Requested: UK	*Request 1* Unlawful coercion; sexual molestation × 2; rape	*Request 2* Mental health; high risk of suicide Initial block on surrender; overturned; extradition allowed based on US assurances; subject to further appeal	*Requests 1 and 2* Delay EAW from Sweden sent November 2010; lapsed during time spent in Ecuadorian Embassy; case involving US request continuing
	Request 2 Requesting: US Requested: UK	*Request 2* Espionage charges × 17; conspiracy to commit computer intrusion		
Dorin Savu	Requesting: Romania Requested: Canada	Fraud; forgery	Fear of persecution; potential torture Significant positive changes in Romania; allowed to make additional submissions to minister; minister's decision not unreasonable	Refugee status Serious offences committed outside of Canada prior to gaining refugee status; no valid reason provided to grant greater protection; minister's decision not unreasonable
Elias Perez	Requesting: Mexico Requested: US	Murder	Violation of CAT; perceived risk of torture, death Court lacked discretion to examine conditions in foreign country; concerns more appropriate for the executive to consider	Rule of non-inquiry Humanitarian exception to the rule of non-inquiry not possible; court lacked discretion to examine conditions in foreign country

Continued

Table 1 *Continued*

Extraditee	Nations Involved	Offence	Primary Issue and Outcome	Secondary Issue and Outcome
Conduct of nations				
Kim Dotcom	Requesting: US Requested: NZ	Conspiracy to commit racketeering; conspiracy to commit copyright infringement; conspiracy to commit money laundering; criminal copyright infringement × 5; wire fraud × 5	Legality of raid, search and seizure by NZ police Warrant unduly broad; legality of evidence from search later endorsed	Double criminality Eligible for surrender on all counts bar single charge of conspiracy to commit money laundering
Hassan Diab	Requesting: France Requested: Canada	Murder × 4; attempted murder × 40; destruction of property	Evidence admissibility and reliability Fifth piece of handwriting analysis could not be rejected as unreliable; magistrate had power to decide admissibility; concerns about evidence derived from torture to be considered after surrender	Continued campaign by France Extradited 2014; never formally charged; released January 2018 due to insufficient evidence; convicted *in absentia* and sentenced to life imprisonment April 2023
Daniel Snedden	Requesting: Croatia Requested: Australia	War crimes × 3	Ability to respond to material sent between nations about specialty Should be given opportunity to review new information; overturned; no evidence of procedural unfairness	Political offence exception in the context of international crime Possible prejudice at trial; overturned

Chapter Outlines

Chapter 1 details the limited individual protections extended to extraditees during the surrender process, which includes potential exposure to the death penalty, whole of life sentences and torture. This chapter emphasises how the process of extradition focuses on the requested state's obligation to comply with a request in light of broader interests of international comity that seek to enhance cooperation in criminal cases. The desire to promote international comity ultimately results in very few successful legal challenges in domestic courts and reveals the substantial degree of judicial deference to executive decision-making and the corresponding limits of individual human rights protections.

Chapter 2 presents the three cases which demonstrate concerns regarding the physical or mental welfare of extraditees. The case descriptions highlight the difficulties extraditees face in successfully challenging an extradition request, even if clear evidence establishes significant harm will occur if surrender is ordered. These issues are examined in detail through the cases of Julian Assange, Dorin Savu and Elias Perez, which were heard by extradition courts in the UK, Canada and the US respectively.

Chapter 3 extends this analysis by reviewing three additional cases where viable concerns regarding the conduct of the requesting and requested nations were largely overlooked by domestic courts considering appeals against extradition. These examples involved legal claims raised by Kim Dotcom in New Zealand (NZ), Hassan Diab in Canada and Daniel Snedden in Australia.

Chapter 4 summarises and links the themes from these cases to core elements of criminal justice procedure. This leads to an exploration of possible reforms that attempt to address the problematic assumptions and outcomes emerging from these cases, with a view to creating a fairer extradition process. These proposals incorporate a defendant-centred approach that enables a more stringent judicial review of the potential harms associated with extradition. The chapter concludes by exploring a more radical reform option involving the harmonisation and universalisation of criminal jurisdiction and the development of a transnational criminal court.

The book concludes with a summary of these issues that seeks to challenge the historically established and dated assumptions about how, why, when and against whom extradition operates. While potentially difficult to implement, the book argues that updated normative assumptions are necessary to promote reform and achieve a truer balance between the rights of nation states and individuals, given the complicated and highly technical nature of contemporary extradition processes.

Chapter 1

EXTRADITION AND INDIVIDUAL PROTECTIONS

Introduction

Extradition is one of the oldest forms of international cooperation and can be traced back to antiquity (Blakesley 1981, 39; Magnuson 2012, 846). The extent to which extradition law has incorporated consideration of the rights of individual suspects has evolved over time. In the mid-eighteenth century, extradition was viewed as an agreement or contract between states on how to deal with fugitive suspects apprehended in another nation's territory (Moore 1891). The idea of extradition as an agreement between nation states actively restricted the enforceable rights of the accused to challenge a request for their surrender. As the types of offences common in extradition requests shifted from political and religious crimes to target military deserters in the eighteenth and nineteenth centuries (Epps 2003), the rationale for core extradition principles also shifted. Double criminality, which requires the offence to be criminalised in both the requesting and requested nations, has always been central to extradition. As this principle matured, extradition increasingly focused on 'the rights of the [extraditee] not to be subject to injustice' in foreign legal systems (Boister 2023, 252). Protections for extraditees continued to develop in the late nineteenth century and now encompass human rights principles enshrined in international conventions, domestically enforced due process rights and other types of individual protections commonly raised in legal challenges to extradition. Principles such as double criminality and specialty, which requires that following surrender an extraditee should not be tried for offences beyond those listed in the request, can also have important functions aimed at protecting people sought to face trial in another nation.

Individual protections within extradition treaties are mainly subject to the requested nation's due process rules or procedures (Anderson 1983; Bloom 2008; Boister 2003; Henning 1999). Domestic due process requirements can vary and often differ from broader international human rights standards (Rose 2002; Ross 2011). Contradictions can also emerge with treaties which aim to detect or control transnational and global crime problems, the domestic incorporation of international human rights requirements and individual protections embedded in the routine operation of the criminal justice systems of requesting states (Arnell 2018; Colquhoun 2000; Dugard and Van den Wyngaert 1998). Therefore, individual rights mechanisms play a limited role during an extradition hearing, which ultimately determines whether the requesting state has a right to the transfer of the extraditee, rather than the individual's right to avoid surrender (Anderson 1983; Arnell 2013; Henning 1999; Piragoff and Kran 1992; Quigley 1990). This is despite 'traditional ideas about comity and sovereignty [giving] way to a renewed interest in fairness' for extraditees (Magnuson 2012, 853). Uncertainty on whether 'global crime-fighting should displace traditional or developing notions of due process and human rights' also affect international and domestic legal processes (Parry 2010, 2003).

This chapter examines how individual rights have emerged in contemporary extradition processes. First, some important protective mechanisms outlined in international human rights treaties which can influence an extradition decision are outlined. Second, the chapter identifies two embedded facets that potentially restrict an extraditee's ability to challenge an extradition request. These are the rule of non-inquiry and the relevance of executive decision-making after a court has ruled on a person's eligibility for surrender. Third, the chapter discusses how these factors combine to create a power imbalance between the requesting and requested nations and individual extraditees. This degree of inequality limits an extraditee's ability to successfully challenge an extradition request.

Limited International Protections

Most international human rights arguments challenging a person's eligibility for extradition emphasise how surrender might 'indirectly lead to an infringement abroad' (Arnell 2018, 872). However, the categories of international human rights protections sufficient to deny extradition are unclear (de Felipe and Martín 2012, 603). Domestic courts are required to speculate on two key issues when considering whether to uphold an extradition request. The first involves the enforceability of human rights instruments in the domestic laws of both the requesting and requested nations. Under laws governing the ratification of international treaties, a human rights protection must be incorporated into domestic law to be legally enforceable (Higgins 2009; MacNaughton and Duger 2020). Second, it is difficult for an extradition court to anticipate the likelihood an extraditee will be mistreated in the requesting nation as international treaties contain no universal standards for evaluating human rights protections. These two problems intersect to account for the varying degrees of regulatory understanding and compliance with international treaty provisions among different nations (Quigley 1990, 427), while illustrating why potential human rights violations will generally only have an indirect bearing on a decision to extradite (Arnell 2018, 872).

Dugard and Van den Wyngaert (1998) and Griffith and Harris (2005) document the main human rights requirements that apply to extradition. These legal protections are derived from various international agreements (examples are identified below), the United Nations (UN) *Model Treaty on Extradition* (1990) and related domestic legislation. They include obligations to prevent the following:

- Any discrimination regarding race, religion, nationality, political opinion, ethnic origin or sex which may have influenced the request or be experienced by the extraditee upon surrender (e.g. *International Covenant on Civil and Political Rights* [ICCPR] 1966).
- A potentially unfair trial, particularly if a conviction occurred *in absentia* and a retrial is not assured (e.g. ICCPR 1966; *Universal Declaration of Human Rights* [UDHR] 1948).
- The imposition of the death penalty (e.g. *Protocol No. 6* 1982 and *Protocol No. 13* 2002 of the *European Convention on Human Rights* [ECHR] 1950; *Second Optional Protocol to the ICCPR* 1989).

International human rights protections under instruments such as the CAT are generally accepted by most nations but are ratified and incorporated into domestic law in very inconsistent ways. Under US law, any legally binding treaty must be fully signed and ratified, although the legal status of treaty provisions between these two phases of implementation remains unclear. This legal uncertainty can prevent ratification or contribute to the outright rejection of an international instrument with political support at the national level (Roberg 2007, 182). Variations in the acceptance of all or part of the terms of international treaties is a symptom of how international law might shape actual or perceived incursions on national sovereignty (Rogoff 1980), which has further ramifications for domestic extradition processes.

Human rights arguments challenging extradition generally focus on the negative impacts of criminal penalties or potential exposure to torture upon surrender. Some of these trends are outlined below.

Death penalty

Extradition cases that can result in the death penalty raise fundamental human rights issues and are generally complex, politically contentious and precedent-setting. One of the most widely cited examples involved German citizen Jens Söering, who was jointly charged with the 1985 murders of the parents of his then girlfriend, Elizabeth Haysom, in Virginia, US. Haysom voluntarily returned from the UK to face trial in Virginia, while Söering challenged his extradition in the UK courts. In 1989, the European Court of Human Rights (ECtHR) ruled that if Söering was surrendered and convicted of murder, he would be unlawfully exposed to the mental anxiety of the death row phenomenon while awaiting execution. This would violate Article 3 of the ECHR, which guarantees the right to be protected from inhuman and degrading treatment (*Söering* 1989). However, the death penalty itself was not deemed to be a clear human rights ground for refusing extradition. This reflects the interests of international comity, where deference is paid to the requesting state's autonomy to implement penalties deemed suitable under its criminal law. Ultimately, Söering was extradited after authorities in Virginia provided assurances the death penalty would not be imposed on conviction. Söering protested his innocence throughout, but was surrendered, convicted and sentenced to life imprisonment in 1990 (Arnell 2013; Ross 2011), then paroled and deported to Germany in December 2019 (Vozzella 2019). This case arguably established an international norm enabling states to block extradition to nations retaining the death penalty (see Botting 2005, 245–53).

Whole of life sentences

Whether whole of life sentences amount to inhuman and degrading treatment deemed sufficient to block extradition is more debatable than the imposition of the death penalty and ultimately depends on cooperative justice agreements between nations (Foster 2015; Labardini 2005). Many challenges to surrender for crimes resulting in life imprisonment without parole are ruled inadmissible or have been found not to violate Article 3 of the ECHR (ECtHR Press Unit 2023). For example, in the case of *Einhorn* (2001), an extraditee contesting extradition to the US from France to serve a sentence of life imprisonment for the murder of his former partner was ruled inadmissible and manifestly ill-founded because the Governor of Pennsylvania retained discretion to commute the sentence, which may later result in parole being granted. Contrastingly, a Tunisian national from Belgium, Trabelsi, who faced surrender to the US on terrorism charges successfully argued extradition would contravene Article 3 of the ECHR because the US had not provided an assurance against an irreducible life sentence (Antinucci 2017; *Trabelsi* 2014). Prior to this ruling, Trabelsi was extradited in violation of an interim ECtHR order in 2013, with the Special Rapporteurs on Torture and the Promotion and Protection of Human Rights and Fundamental Freedoms while Countering

Terrorism stating in December 2020 that his mental health had deteriorated severely while in continued solitary confinement, which magnified the risk of further exposure to torture and other ill-treatment (Melzer and Aoláin 2020).

Exposure to torture

Extraditees can also invoke specific international human rights agreements to challenge surrender. While most extradition treaties do not explicitly prohibit extradition if torture is likely to occur after surrender, many countries recognise the human rights record of a requesting country can justify refusing extradition under the CAT (Abbell 2010, 130; Johnston 2011, 4). Article 1 of the CAT defines torture as:

> any act by which severe pain or suffering, whether physical or mental, is intentionally inflicted on a person for such purposes as obtaining from him or a third person information or a confession, punishing him for an act he or a third person has committed or is suspected of having committed, or intimidating or coercing him or a third person, or for any reason based on discrimination of any kind, when such pain or suffering is inflicted by or at the instigation of or with the consent or acquiescence of a public official or other person acting in an official capacity. It does not include pain or suffering arising only from, inherent in or incidental to lawful sanctions.

Human rights arguments have blocked extradition where lengthy mandatory sentences, poor prison conditions and 'death row anguish' could be experienced by a surrendered person (Dugard and Van den Wyngaert 1998). Article 3 of the CAT provides clear justification for such protection:

1. No State Party shall expel, return ("refouler") or extradite a person to another State where there are substantial grounds for believing that he would be in danger of being subjected to torture.
2. For the purpose of determining whether there are such grounds, the competent authorities shall take into account all relevant considerations including, where applicable, the existence in the State concerned of a consistent pattern of gross, flagrant or mass violations of human rights.

The Office of the High Commissioner for Human Rights (1997) has indicated the protections under Article 3 of the CAT should be limited to cases where there are 'substantial grounds' for believing an extraditee would experience torture from a public official after being expelled, returned or extradited to a requesting state, or any other country. When examining potential exposure to torture as a possible reason to reject an extradition request on human rights grounds, courts must consider the following:

- The burden of proof rests with the individual to provide a factual basis sufficient to convince the state examining the request that extradition should be denied.
- The risk of torture must be highly probable and more than a theoretical possibility.
- The extraditee must provide substantial grounds indicating a personal and present danger of being tortured if extradited.

In other words, Article 3 will only be invoked to bar extradition if the extraditee can provide credible evidence, with no factual inconsistencies, that establishes:

- A consistent pattern of human rights violations in the requesting country.
- Prior experiences of torture or maltreatment, with ongoing effects, supported by medical or other independent evidence.
- Engagement in political or other activities within or outside the requesting state that increases their risk of exposure to torture.

Transnational crime control treaties

Several transnational crime control treaties contain specific provisions relating to extradition. For example, the *Convention on Cybercrime* (2001), also known as the *Budapest Convention*, seeks to enhance multinational cooperation by providing the jurisdictional basis for extradition for several specified online offences. These provisions introduce 'jurisdictional requirements that supplement, and in some cases replace, those forged through pre-existing bilateral and multilateral extradition arrangements that are incorporated into national laws' (Kennedy and Warren 2020, 1–2), while enabling a streamlined extradition process for certain online offences that can result in a minimum term of imprisonment of 12 months (Clough 2014). Article 24(6) also incorporates the principle of *aut dedere aut judicare*, which requires parties to 'extradite or prosecute'. However, the *Budapest Convention* is largely silent on the human rights implications of extradition in cases of transnational cyber offending.

The Rule of Non-Inquiry and Power of the Executive

Ultimately, the surrender of an extraditee requires a decision by the executive branch of government after a court has ruled on a person's extraditability.

This procedure raises concerns about the centrality of political comity in extradition decisions and highlights the influence of diplomatic and economic relationships between states, which are particularly salient in complex or emotive criminal cases. These factors often outweigh concerns over the human rights impacts of surrender on the extraditee.

Courts are central in determining the impacts of surrender and criminal prosecution on extraditees. Nevertheless, courts scrutinising human rights or other protective arguments against extradition are often hampered by the rule of non-inquiry. Executive decision-making can also override court rulings aimed at protecting an extraditee's rights, which can further limit consideration of the prospects of ill-treatment in a requesting state. Both the rule of non-inquiry and the executive power to override a judicial ruling on human rights grounds can result in decisions that favour the political interests of the requesting nation (Magnuson 2012; Warren and Palmer 2015), without considering due process rules, procedures or any potential mistreatment of the extraditee. This structure has reinforced the development of several rules that stipulate any potential mistreatment must be extreme, targeted and in contradiction to broad national values of decency and good conscience before any human rights arguments will be considered (Bassiouni 2014; Dugard and Van den Wyngaert 1998; Harrington 2005). Executive decision-making also plays a role in granting political assurances and plea deals which can be used to advance extradition cases, with any potential unfairness and other related individual rights issues associated with these approaches rarely examined.

The rule of non-inquiry

The rule of non-inquiry is a convention rather than a binding law of extradition. This principle determines it is neither necessary nor appropriate for courts to investigate the operation of criminal justice systems in requesting countries (Arnell 2013; Bassiouni 2014; King 2015; Pyle 2001; Quigley 1996; Sullivan 1991). The rule of non-inquiry 'has been developed in deference to the sovereignty of the requesting state' (Bassiouni 2014, 633). It reinforces the centrality of the contract theory of treaty relations by placing mutual trust in the development and enforcement of terms contained in bi- and multilateral extradition arrangements, and the enforcement of accepted due process protections in the criminal justice systems of requesting states. Removing this rule would arguably convert an extradition hearing into a comparative examination of the nuances of justice administration in the requesting state, rather than a process for determining the basic standards for the surrender of extraditees under the terms of politically negotiated treaties. In other words, the rule of non-inquiry has significant potential to compromise judicial consideration of the rights and welfare of extraditees.

The rule of non-inquiry recognises that domestic extradition courts should uphold a 'mandate of institutional neutrality' by not examining the conditions of justice administration in the requesting nation (Murchison 2007, 304). Problematic issues in the requesting country can involve the availability of competent legal representation, the circumstances of collecting and legally challenging prosecution evidence, or possible maltreatment, which includes exposure to overcrowding or medical neglect during pretrial or post-conviction detention. While cases invoking the rule of non-inquiry 'have not been uniform in their approach' (Quigley 1990, 415), it is considered a fundamental element of US extradition law. In most other jurisdictions, the rule is implied by entry into a bi- or multilateral extradition or crime control treaty. In Australia, it is expressed through the principle that the fairness of an extradition request will be judged on Australian legal standards (*Adamas* 2013). Ultimately, extradition courts will avoid questioning the processes of criminal justice administration in a requesting state because to do so would contradict its sovereign power and the centrality of the state-based system of transnational justice cooperation (Magnuson 2012, 886).

The rule of non-inquiry generally favours a state's obligation to extradite (Parry 2010). This can create significant problems (Blakesley 2000) and 'unjust surrenders' (Pyle 2001, 301). For example, Pyle (2001, 128–29) documents the case of Joao F. Normano, a Jewish professor at Harvard University who was sought by Germany in 1933 for fraud. The US State Department authorised Normano's surrender without considering whether he would receive a fair trial under the Nazi criminal justice regime. In invoking the rule of non-inquiry, the US court stated that Hitler's persecution of Jewish people:

> ought not to influence the decision. Whatever may be the situation in Germany, the Extradition Treaty between that government and the United States is still in full force, and it is the duty of the court to uphold and respect it. (*Normano* 1934, 330–31)

A technical delay with the case, rather than any clear human rights arguments, ultimately led to Normano's release in the US (*Normano* 1934; Pyle 2001, 129; Sullivan 1991, 117).

Since the 1960s, greater emphasis on protecting individual human rights in light of the atrocities of World War II has generated calls to replace the rule of non-inquiry (Epps 2003, 380; Zelinsky 2009). This would enable extradition courts to examine the requesting state's criminal justice processes when the extraditee can present evidence establishing a likelihood of exposure to mistreatment, impropriety or procedural failings considered to be 'antipathetic to a [...] court's sense of decency' (*Gallina* 1960, para. 79; Sullivan 1991).

Executive decision-making after judicial review

The High Court of Australia has ruled that extradition is primarily an executive act (*Vasiljkovic* 2006a). This means the role of an extradition court is confined to screening the merits of a request through limited inquiry into the human rights implications of the person's surrender, as these issues are commonly dealt with during treaty negotiations or on a case-by-case basis following a judicial ruling on extraditability (Bassiouni 2008; King 2015; Parry 2010; Van Cleave 1999). It is rare for the executive to rule against surrender (Blakesley 1980). However, protective elements can be built into an extradition treaty, such as Article VIII of the *Treaty on Extradition between Australia and the United States of America* (1976). This requirement stipulates that if the offence is subject to the death penalty which is not a sentencing option in the requested state, the requested state 'may recommend to the requesting State that any punishment imposed for any of those offences be a less severe punishment'. Notably, the word 'may' indicates such a recommendation is discretionary rather than binding on the executive.

Executive discretion can overturn a judicial ruling favouring extradition when there is concern about an extraditee's welfare. This occurred in the English case involving Gary McKinnon (Mann et al. 2018). In 2002, the US indicted McKinnon for offences involving the unlawful alteration, deletion, scanning or copying of classified Army, Naval, Air Force and NASA online account details which allegedly occurred via his home computer in London (*McKinnon* 2002a, 2002b). McKinnon raised several arguments when challenging his extradition, which included suggestions he was unfairly targeted by US authorities for his political beliefs, the impact of surrender on his mental health as a person diagnosed with autism spectrum disorder and the coercive nature of a US plea deal aimed at securing his surrender. UK extradition courts rejected these arguments and McKinnon's surrender was ordered in July 2006 (*McKinnon* 2007). Several unsuccessful legal appeals ensued before the then Home Secretary Theresa May announced in October 2012 that extradition would not proceed due to McKinnon's high risk of suicide and the 'flawed and unlawful reasoning' of the UK courts, which rejected his claims under the UK's *Human Rights Act* (1998) (May 2012).

However, cases like McKinnon's are rare and it is considered 'irresponsible and [...] anachronistic' for an extraditee's human rights to be upheld through a discretionary decision of the executive branch of government (Murchison 2007, 313). This is because extradition is 'one of those judicially protected guarantees of liberty and fairness the executive is forever trying to erode' (Pyle 2001, 1). Nevertheless, courts often find arguments about individual rights violations 'lie outside their jurisdiction and [are] a matter for executive decision' (Anderson 1983, 153), even though it is becoming 'increasingly difficult [...] for judges to ignore the consequences of certifying extradition to a country with a poor human rights record' (Shea 1992, 131).

Assurances and plea deals

In cases involving the death penalty, assurances often facilitate surrender of the extraditee to face lower charges that will result in a term of imprisonment on conviction. In *Söering* (1989), the assurances against the imposition of the death penalty given by the US to the UK played a key role in enabling surrender. However, the political nature of assurances affirms the power of the executive to influence extradition outcomes.

The Canadian case involving Sebastian Burns and Atif Rafay produced a similar outcome (*Burns* 2001). In July 1994, Rafay's mother, father and sister were bludgeoned to death in an apparent burglary in their home in the US state of Washington. Burns and Rafay returned to Canada, where Burns admitted to undercover officers of the Royal Canadian Mounted Police that he had committed the murders in Rafay's presence. Following their arrest, a Canadian magistrate ruled both were eligible for surrender despite potential exposure to the death penalty under the criminal law in Washington.

Burns and Rafay submitted documentation to the executive arguing there was a legal requirement for the Canadian government to seek assurances against the imposition of the death penalty under sections 6(1), 7 and 12 of the *Canadian Charter of Rights and Freedoms (Canadian Charter)* (1982), and in line with Article 6 of the *Treaty on Extradition Between the Government of Canada and the Government of the United States* (1976) (Harvie and Foster 2005, 313). Section 6(1) of the *Canadian Charter* states that Canadian citizens have the right to enter or remain in Canada and should not be expelled by the government with the risk of never returning, while section 7 states that everyone has the right to life, liberty and security and section 12 prohibits cruel and unusual treatment or punishment by the state. It was also claimed assurances against the death penalty were necessary because Burns and Rafay were only 18 years of age at the time of the offences. However, the Minister of Justice signed an unconditional surrender warrant enabling both co-accused to face three counts of aggravated first-degree murder in Washington, with assurances only deemed necessary 'where the particular facts of the case warrant a special exercise of discretion' (*Burns* 2001, 18).

Burns and Rafay appealed and successfully argued the decision not to utilise the discretionary power to seek assurances against the death penalty violated section 6(1) of the *Canadian Charter* because they would be forced out of Canada and, if executed, could not exercise their right to return (Harvie and Foster 2005, 314). The executive decision was also deemed to contravene Article 6 of the extradition treaty between Canada and the US, which can bar surrender if domestic legislation in the requested state does not sanction the death penalty. After this ruling, US authorities provided assurances to the Canadian government that Burns and Rafay would not be exposed to the death penalty, and they were ultimately extradited to face trial in Washington. Both were convicted in 2004 and sentenced to life imprisonment without the possibility of parole. Notably, the Canadian government must now seek assurances against the death penalty as a condition of extradition to any country (Rose 2002, 207).

Plea deals to secure an extraditee's surrender operate in a similar way to political assurances. While an executive decision ultimately prevented McKinnon's extradition, between November 2002 and April 2003 the US attempted to expedite his voluntary surrender in exchange for a plea of guilty on two charges. This would have required McKinnon to pay between US$400,000 and US$1 million in restitution to the US government and waive all his appeal rights under the premise of being returned to the UK under the US and UK prisoner transfer agreement after serving a three- to four-year term of imprisonment in the US (Mann et al. 2018; *McKinnon* 2007). If McKinnon rejected this offer, US prosecutors would argue for a maximum of eight to ten years imprisonment for each charge to be served in a high-security prison, with only 15% sentence remission and no guarantee of repatriation (*McKinnon* 2008). McKinnon ultimately rejected this deal and challenged his extradition in the UK courts.

These cases demonstrate executive assurances and plea bargains can have significant impacts on an extraditee's rights, with political comity potentially playing a key role in the process of certifying extradition. In particular, assurances reflect the impact of political action that reinforces the quasi-legal status of extradition, based on the requesting state's primary aim of securing an extraditee's surrender (*Giese* 2015, para. 14).

A Complicated Relationship

Theoretically, extradition hearings should evenly balance the varying national and individual human rights issues that arise in each case (Blakesley 1980). However, the legal status of the rule of non-inquiry and the political nature of executive decision-making complicate these issues, particularly when human rights and due process standards in requesting nations are questionable. In theory, concerns over whether an individual's basic human rights will be protected can block extradition entirely or lead to conditional surrender being sanctioned by an extradition court or the executive. However, most extradition decisions focus on the requested state's obligation to transfer the extraditee, rather than the potential harms associated with surrender. This emphasis is strengthened by the tendency for extradition courts to defer to decisions of the executive (Arnell 2013; Henning 1999; Piragoff and Kran 1992). This means extradition is often considered:

> an aspect of international relations in which states, not individuals, are the only rights holders. This nation-centered, and therefore executive-centered, approach ha[s] the unfortunate effect of denigrating the extent to which surrender of persons to foreign governments also raises issues of judicial independence, executive authority, individual liberty, and due process of law. (Pyle 2001, 2)

This pattern results in the 'subordination of individual rights to [international] policy interests' (Bifani 1993, 630), which is otherwise termed international comity. Comity reinforces the historic view that individual human rights are considered 'inconvenient' barriers to international justice cooperation and transnational crime control (Dugard and Van den Wyngaert 1998; Murchison 2007, 296). In fact, available research indicates national courts tend to have a 'narrow view of individual rights' (Bifani 1993, 677) and are likely to interpret extradition treaties to promote cooperative transnational justice, law enforcement and crime control objectives (Leeson 1996; Williams 1992).

This emphasis persists due to the very low success rate of individual rights arguments in extradition cases (Anderson 1983; Arnell 2013; Harrington 2005; Merry 2006; Piragoff and Kran 1992). The consistent trend towards granting requests (Blakesley 2008; Magnuson 2012) stems from the high 'precedential stakes' associated with extradition cases (Cullen and Burgess 2015, 234). The high evidentiary thresholds for establishing that an extraditee will likely face a rights violation if surrendered also reinforces the centrality of the rule of non-inquiry. This degree of circularity to extradition law means extraditees must produce clear and substantial proof they will experience direct harm if surrendered. However, due to the rule of non-inquiry, extraditees are restricted in the evidence they can submit, which often creates situations where courts emphasise there is a lack of sufficient proof to bar extradition on human rights grounds (Arnell 2013; Parry 2010).

For example, UK and Irish courts have been reluctant to accept human rights arguments to block the surrender of extraditees diagnosed with autism spectrum disorders who have been sought for charges of online offending in the US, including McKinnon (Mann et al. 2018). Mann and Warren (2018, 251) emphasise that this approach reinforces 'the carceral rather than procedural or human rights impacts in domestic extradition' theory and practice by using the case of Gary Davis. Davis was sought for extradition by the US from Ireland on charges stemming from his role as an administrator of the *Silk Road* dark web cryptomarket, a globally accessible platform for organising transactions to sell and purchase illicit drugs that operated from the US. Davis argued his surrender could magnify the effects of his autism and depression, which could amount to inhuman and degrading treatment under Articles 3 and 8 of the ECHR. However, the UK High Court was satisfied the US prison system could implement appropriate measures to protect Davis's health (*Davis* 2016; Mann and Warren 2018), and he was surrendered, convicted and sentenced to 78 months of imprisonment in July 2019 (US Attorney's Office, Southern District of New York 2019).

While the number of extradition cases that might involve a proven physical or procedural risk to extraditees is small (Parry 2010), the pattern of granting limited judicial relief for human rights claims persists. National courts commonly reject specific arguments associated with widely accepted international human rights agreements such as the CAT and allegations involving the potential violation of due process rights in requesting states that include police misconduct, questionable criminal court procedures and onerous prison conditions. Other arguments, such as those related to the admissibility and reliability of evidence, are also commonly unsuccessful and deemed by extradition courts to be more appropriate for consideration in a criminal trial following surrender. Chapters 2 and 3 examine each of these issues in more detail.

Conclusion

This chapter explored the complexities which exist when attempting to ensure human rights and individual protections are recognised in extradition law. Tensions between international and domestic legal and criminal justice processes, the complex relationship between the executive and judiciary, the operation of the rule of non-inquiry and high evidentiary standards to establish viable human rights claims all combine to limit the ability of extraditees to avoid surrender. These embedded elements of extradition law actively restrict detailed consideration of protective international and domestic human rights arguments when an extradition request is challenged. These issues are especially prominent in the cases discussed in the following two chapters.

Chapter 2

EXTRADITION IN PRACTICE: THE WELFARE OF EXTRADITEES

Introduction

This chapter describes three cases involving legal claims by extraditees that their surrender would have serious consequences on their physical and mental health. In the case of Julian Assange, extensive delays have contributed to his deteriorating mental health and a high risk of suicide if he is surrendered to the US to face numerous charges of espionage. The case of Dorin Savu introduced evidence that surrender would raise potential exposure to torture in the requesting state, while the extradition proceedings considered the significance of his status and rights as a refugee in Canada. The case of Elias Perez raised arguments against extradition that focused on his potential exposure to violations of the CAT if he was surrendered to face trial in Mexico and related arguments involving the rule of non-inquiry. The individual rights arguments in all of these cases were largely rejected because courts considering the request were willing to support the overarching authority of the requesting nation to prosecute each suspect for various crimes. The chapter will describe key factual and legal details raised in each case and demonstrate how they reveal the need for reform to the process of extradition given the limited recognition of the obligation to protect the rights of extraditees, as well as their physical and mental welfare.

Julian Assange, Mental Health and Delay

Australian citizen Julian Assange's attempts to avoid extradition from the UK, first to Sweden to face questioning over alleged sexual offences and then the US on serious espionage charges, spanned a total of 13 years. This includes seven years of self-imposed exile in the Ecuadorian Embassy in London to avoid surrender to Sweden, largely due to fears he would be unlawfully sent to the US despite prohibitions against surrender to third-party states in extradition treaties. Assange has repeatedly claimed the legal processes for extradition would lead to his unlawful transfer to the US, resulting in a possible maximum term of 175 years in prison (Australian Associated Press 2021). His charges are linked to the activities of WikiLeaks, a website launched in Sweden by Assange in 2006 as a forum for maintaining accountability for governments throughout the world through the 'principled leaking' of confidential documents (Karhula 2011, 1). WikiLeaks published hundreds of thousands of US documents associated with military operations in Afghanistan and Iraq, which led to the conviction and eventual commutation of the sentence of Chelsea Manning, an intelligence officer with the US military who provided sensitive files to Assange (Allely et al. 2022, 630). While concerned about the fairness of any trial in the US given the political sensitivity associated with the disclosure of contentious offshore military activities, Assange has argued surrender would exacerbate various mental health conditions that have either emerged or worsened during his extended period in confinement since establishing WikiLeaks, including recurrent depression, post-traumatic stress disorder and autism spectrum disorder (Allely et al. 2022).

Since 2010, English courts have examined the extradition attempts by Sweden and the US several times. These proceedings include the following:

- A successful bail application while awaiting an extradition decision to face interrogation in Sweden on sexual assault allegations (*Assange* 2010).
- An unsuccessful appeal against the extradition certification to Sweden (*Assange* 2011).
- An unsuccessful application to reopen the dismissal of the previous appeal (*Assange* 2012).
- A finding of ineligibility for extradition to the US on espionage charges due to his poor mental health and high risk of suicide (*Assange* 2021a).
- The endorsement of an appeal against his ineligibility for extradition by the US (*Assange* 2021b).
- A finding quashing the denial of extradition due to the acceptance of an extensive list of protective assurances provided by US justice authorities (*Assange* 2021c). Assange has successfully challenged this decision, which allows further scrutiny of the assurances provided by the US government in the UK courts (Stuart 2024).

These cases highlight the political nature of extradition law, which commonly overshadows legal consideration of an individual's rights. For example, although Assange initially agreed to provide evidence to Swedish prosecutors relating to the sexual assault charges, English courts reviewing the merits of Sweden's request under the EAW found sufficient evidence to justify his surrender for questioning. The more serious impacts of alleged national security violations raised by the US highlight the sensitive nature of many extradition requests and continued concerns about the operation of WikiLeaks, including coordinated efforts to ensure government transparency, civil liberties, free speech and freedom of information in the digital age. Most English judicial rulings prioritised the importance of England's international comity with Sweden and the US. This is despite concerns about fairness if an individual is surrendered to face questioning rather than prosecution, which was the case with the Swedish request, or the clear risks surrender poses to Assange's physical and mental health in regard to the US request. The various elements of this case highlight the problematic impacts of delay and the potential lack of neutrality in dealing with allegations of complex forms of electronic crime that affect national security.

Swedish EAW request

In 2011, Swedish prosecutors asked the UK to surrender Assange for questioning during an investigation into four sexual assault allegations that included one count of rape (Allely et al. 2022). The UN Special Rapporteur on Torture has subsequently viewed the English decisions to surrender Assange under the EAW process (*Assange* 2011, 2012) as an example of 'deference to political interests' (Melzer 2022, 212). This is because the chief Swedish prosecutor, rather than a judicial authority, sought the EAW simply to question Assange, rather than to face a criminal trial or formally administered sentence under Swedish law. Throughout, it appears Assange was willing to respond to questions before he was permitted to leave Sweden for England in October 2010, or via video link as the extradition proceedings were being heard by the English courts.

Extradition to Sweden was certified by England in February 2011 while Assange was on conditional bail (*Assange* 2010, 2011, 2012). Prior to appealing these decisions in the ECtHR and fearing either lawful or unlawful transfer by Sweden to the US, Assange entered the Ecuadorian Embassy in London in June 2012, where he remained for over seven years (Warren and Palmer 2015, 373–74). Assange's decision to seek diplomatic asylum in the Ecuadorian Embassy prior to the commencement of appeals to the ECtHR effectively barred final consideration of the validity of the Swedish EAW request. However, the English court orders granting Assange's surrender to face questioning, rather than a formal trial, are considered disproportionate in comparison to his protected rights under the ECHR.

In 2015, the Working Group on Arbitrary Detention of the Human Rights Council found Assange's detention in England contravened the UDHR and the ICCPR. However, these findings had no bearing on future judicial decisions regarding the request under the EAW or for the breach of bail under English law. In February 2018, it was determined the English arrest warrant linked to Assange's breach of bail, which was violated when he entered the Ecuadorian Embassy, should continue (*Assange* 2018a). Ecuador subsequently revoked Assange's asylum after accusations he leaked information about the Ecuadorian president's personal life, and he was arrested by English police in April 2019 for breach of bail (ABC News 2019). Assange was convicted for this offence in the Southwark Crown Court in May 2019 and sentenced to 50 weeks imprisonment (*Assange* 2019a). After ceasing preliminary investigations into the sexual assault charges while Assange was in the embassy, Swedish prosecutors discontinued all proceedings in November 2019 as the 'witnesses' memories had faded' after almost a decade since the allegations first emerged (Quinn 2019).

Contesting US extradition

While English courts were finalising the decision on Assange's bail violation in 2019, several indictments were issued alleging the publication of confidential government files on WikiLeaks involved criminal offending that compromised US national security (*Assange* 2018b, 2019b, 2020). Each indictment alleged Assange encouraged members of a global online hacking network to provide him with classified information to be posted on WikiLeaks without government permission, and hence unlawfully. The final 18-count criminal indictment accused Assange of multiple breaches of the US *Espionage Act* (1917), including conspiracy to obtain and disclose national defence information, obtaining national defence information, disclosure of national defence information and conspiracy to commit computer intrusions.

Assange's first challenge to extradition under this US indictment was upheld in January 2021. The English court agreed with Assange's claim because he provided compelling evidence that his mental condition was 'such that it would be oppressive to extradite him to the U.S.' (*Assange* 2021a, para. 363). Medical opinions indicated Assange had a long history of autism spectrum disorder and other mental health conditions that deteriorated during his time in the Ecuadorian Embassy, and placed him at a high risk of self-harm and suicide. This initial ruling found that due to the conditions in the US prison system, Assange's mental health 'would deteriorate causing him to commit suicide with the "single minded determination" of his autism spectrum disorder' (*Assange* 2021a, para. 362). English District Judge Vanessa Baraitser determined there would be a 'real risk that [Assange] will be kept in [...] near isolated conditions', which would prevent him from accessing necessary support while in prison, including family and friends, a Samaritans phoneline and a mental health practitioner from HMP Belmarsh in England with whom he had developed a positive and supportive relationship (*Assange* 2021a, para. 357).

An appeal against this decision by the US was allowed in August 2021 to examine errors of law, concerns about potentially misleading evidence from one of Assange's supporting psychiatric experts and the viability of US assurances to offer treatment for his mental health conditions (*Assange* 2021b). This appeal was upheld, and in December 2021, it was decided Assange was eligible for extradition (*Assange* 2021c). The decision was contingent on the US complying with several assurances it put forward to support its appeal. These included ensuring Assange would not be subject to any special imprisonment measure and would be provided 'any such clinical and psychological treatment as is recommended by a qualified treating clinician employed or retained by the prison where he is held in custody' (*Assange* 2021c, para. 30). The US also agreed that if convicted, Assange could be transferred to Australia to serve his sentence if a workable arrangement could be made with the Australian government. These assurances appear central to the decision supporting the US extradition request, despite clear evidence Assange's autism spectrum disorder and other serious mental health conditions can magnify his already high risk of suicide.

This outcome mirrors many examples where the health concerns of extraditees are given reduced priority compared with the obligation to uphold international comity by ordering surrender. In fact, arguments seeking to recognise the mental health of extraditees often only block extradition 'for a relatively short time' (Arnell 2019, 343). Ultimately, 'the onus falls upon the requested person to establish that it would be oppressive or unjust to extradite because of mental or physical health' (Arnell 2019, 349). For example, advanced age and serious health complications, including cancer and having to care for an ailing spouse, were considered insufficient to bar an elderly extraditee's surrender to the US to face fraud charges (*Norris* 2010). Similarly, in *Badesha* (2017), the Supreme Court of Canada found that multiple health conditions and potential exposure to torture were insufficient to bar the surrender of a man aged 70 years and a woman aged 66 years who were sought to face trial in India for murder and conspiracy to murder that stemmed from a violent honour killing. The acceptance of various assurances offered by India was ultimately sufficient in convincing both the Canadian Supreme Court and the executive that the extraditees would be protected upon their surrender. Finally, in *Hilton* (2013a, 2013b, 2014), an extraditee who was sought by the UK to face charges of attempted murder failed to show that his poor mental health and risk of suicide were sufficient to bar extradition. These rulings support Magnuson's (2012) argument that the existence of an extradition treaty creates a presumption of surrender, even if there are clear physical or mental health risks to individual extraditees.

At the time of writing, Assange has foregone his remaining appeals through the English courts and potentially in the ECtHR (Rebaza and Said-Moorhouse 2023), by agreeing 'to plead guilty to a single criminal count of conspiring to obtain and disclose classified US national defence documents' (Pilkington 2024). Notably, the deal came after the Australian government began to advocate more rigorously for Assange's release (Knott 2023), with his sentence under US jurisdiction likely to result in no further jail time and his immediate return to Australia (Pilkington 2024). This saga highlights the complex political factors underpinning the law of extradition, including the diplomatic nature of assurances and plea deals, which are particularly stark given the national security concerns surrounding Assange's alleged offending in the US and the symbolic value of his admission of guilt.

Dorin Savu, Torture and Refugee Status

Extradition shares many commonalities with immigration, deportation and asylum. In all cases, national courts and executive decision-makers consider the legal authority and obligation to remove an individual from a nation, which by implication erodes a person's legal rights in their geographic location. The case of Dorin Savu explored the complicated, although under-researched, intersection and conflict between extradition and a person's status as a refugee. This case also raised repeated allegations that Savu would be exposed to torture and persecution if surrendered to Romania to serve a five-year and six-month term of imprisonment for fraud and forgery relating to the unlawful sale of gasoline.

In December 2000, the two convictions against Savu were quashed and a new trial was ordered. However, prior to the start of the second trial in May 2001, Savu and his family left Romania for Canada. They were granted refugee status in July 2002 due to their fear of persecution as members of the Roma gypsy minority. In April 2004, they were granted permanent residency in Canada. However, in November 2002, Savu was convicted *in absentia* during a second trial in Romania and was then sought for extradition, which was granted in October 2008 (*Savu* 2008).

Convention Relating to the Status of Refugees (1951)

The legal status of the protections under the international *Convention Relating to the Status of Refugees (Refugee Convention)* (1951) in Canada is central to this case.

A core principle of the *Refugee Convention* is that a refugee should not be returned or 'refouled' to a country where they would face serious threats to life or freedom. Despite arguments and evidence illustrating Savu's fear of persecution in Romania, including the realistic prospect of ill-treatment and torture, the Canadian executive made an order for his extradition in February 2009. The reasoning for this order indicated Savu was not protected under the *Refugee Convention* because Article (1)(F)(b) states the prohibition on refoulment:

> shall not apply to any person with respect to whom there are serious reasons for considering he has committed a serious non-political crime outside the country of refuge prior to his admission to that country as a refugee.

The Canadian extradition decision also found Savu faced no serious risk of persecution because significant changes to the operation of the criminal justice system had occurred in Romania since he had left with his family. These changes were documented by Citizenship and Immigration Canada and submitted for consideration to the Minister of Justice when ordering Savu's extradition.

As Savu's appeals proceeded through the Canadian courts, two significant cases were decided that clarified the method of analysis to be used when decisions relating to the extradition of a refugee arise (*Németh* 2010; *Gavrila* 2010). These cases found the Canadian government could extradite refugees if a proper analysis under section 44 of the *Extradition Act* (1999) was conducted. This legislative requirement specifies mandatory grounds for the refusal of surrender. These include a blanket prohibition on surrender if it is possible the extraditee will be exposed to the death penalty in the requesting state, or the prospect that:

(a) the surrender would be unjust or oppressive having regard to all the relevant circumstances.

(b) the request for extradition is made for the purpose of prosecuting or punishing the person by reason of their race, religion, nationality, ethnic origin, language, colour, political opinion, sex, sexual orientation, age, mental or physical disability or status or that the person's position may be prejudiced for any of those reasons.

After examining these cases, Savu was allowed to make additional submissions to the Minister of Justice which reiterated prior arguments that his ill-treatment in Romania would result in torture because he was a Roma gypsy.

However, the Minister of Justice upheld Romania's request and ordered Savu's extradition.

In 2013, Savu argued the minister had committed an error and exceeded jurisdiction when concluding the protections under the *Refugee Convention* did not apply under Canadian domestic law. This argument was supported by the previous decision of the Canadian Immigration and Refugee Board, which granted Savu asylum in Canada due to the risks he would face if returned to Romania. It was argued this reasoning should be extended to prevent his extradition. However, the court found the minister's decision to order extradition was reasonable because Savu did not provide:

> any valid reason for granting greater protection to a person who has committed a serious crime in his country of origin and who has already been granted asylum, than to a person who has committed the same crime, but whose application is pending at the time of the initiation of the extradition proceedings. (*Savu* 2013a, para. 71)

Savu was released pending appeal (*Savu* 2013b) which was ultimately dismissed in September 2013 (*Savu* 2013c). However, this ruling did not include information about why the application was dismissed. Additional information about the extradition proceedings or surrender of Savu was unavailable at the time of writing.

An uncommon but concerning issue

Extradition cases involving an individual who has sought refuge from the requesting country, such as Savu, are relatively uncommon. However, these cases can emerge in criminal prosecutions involving large-scale international atrocities where there is a genuine fear a refugee might be persecuted if subject to an extradition request and ordered to be surrendered despite the principle of non-refoulment (Palmer 2015). A similar issue arises when an extraditee fears deportation or transfer to a third country following the finalisation of their case in the requesting nation. This was Assange's concern with potential surrender to Sweden under the EAW, which created a risk he would be forwarded to the US, with or without the opportunity to defend his surrender.

In *Bulaman* (2015), the extraditee was granted refugee status and permanent residency in Canada in 2009. In February 2013, he was sought for extradition by the US to face charges of conspiracy to traffic 100 kilograms of cocaine and possession of cocaine for the purpose of trafficking. Despite arguing his surrender would involve 'an indirect return to Turkey [his country of origin] where the danger of persecution is patent, which has the effect of rendering his extradition unfair, [and] tyrannical' (*Bulaman* 2015, para. 44), Bulaman was extradited to the US where he pled guilty and was sentenced to a 14-year imprisonment term (US Attorney's Office, District of New Jersey 2017). Other cases also highlight the limited impact of refugee status when attempting to challenge an extradition request (*Adam* 2014; *Churuk* 2013; *Igwe* 2014; *Suarez* 2014; *Talashkova* 2014).

Orchard (2017) emphasises the long history of attempts to protect refugees under both international and domestic laws, including the emergence of a classification of 'political refugees' and the role of extradition law as a protective aspect of transnational justice cooperation. However, these approaches pre-dated the current *Refugee Convention* and focused primarily on the political offence exception which blocked the extradition of political refugees. The Savu case, and others like it, demonstrates how the types of arguments associated with refugee status have shifted in recent decades by focusing on potential human rights violations associated with the risk of physical mistreatment, rather than broader notions of political persecution. Even when a widely accepted international agreement such as the *Refugee Convention* is applicable, it is difficult for extraditees to produce enough evidence to uphold their claims in the courts of requested nations, which are limited in terms of the types of inquiries and decisions they can make due to the rule of non-inquiry.

Elias Perez, the CAT and the Rule of Non-Inquiry

Perez (2016a) involved an allegation that Elias Perez pulled his car in front of a taxi, exited with a gun and fired three shots, killing the passenger. During the extradition certification hearing, Perez argued he would be tortured and killed if returned to Mexico which would violate his human rights protections under the CAT. Perez testified in the US extradition court that the Mexican government could not ensure his protection if extradition was ordered, as he had received death threats, his son-in-law had been killed and his brother had been shot. However, the US court stated the rule of non-inquiry prevented it from considering any prospect of an extraditee's future mistreatment by a foreign state, despite the seriousness of the claims and the evidence supporting Perez's concerns. The court reasoned that these allegations were considered more appropriate to address during the executive phase of the extradition process.

On appeal in *Perez* (2016b), it was argued a humanitarian exception to the rule of non-inquiry could be made due to the high likelihood Perez would be tortured or murdered if returned to Mexico, which again raised potential violations of the CAT. However, the court denied this appeal, reiterating that it lacked the discretion to examine the potential treatment of extraditees surrendered to a foreign country. Specifically, the ruling emphasised that 'humanitarian claims do not give rise to habeas relief from extradition' and the court 'should not overstep the clear bounds of its jurisdiction to create such an exception in this case' (*Perez* 2016b, 17).

A motion to stay the extradition proceedings pending a second petition for *habeas corpus* was denied in 2017. The court found this petition would be unlikely to succeed, as Perez failed to show irreparable injury would occur to him without a stay, and the public interest worked against his claim (*Perez* 2017a). The second writ of *habeas corpus* was subsequently dismissed as moot as Perez was extradited on 17 February 2017 (*Perez* 2017b). Further information about proceedings following extradition was unavailable.

A powerful blocking mechanism

The rulings against Perez demonstrate how the rule of non-inquiry places the primary responsibility for preserving the human rights of the extraditee onto the requesting nation after surrender is ordered. Significantly, no US court has 'made an exception to the rule of non-inquiry' (*Hilton* 2013b, 8). A judge in one US case stated this 'rule has a narrow scope and is typically cited only to bar inquiry into humanitarian concerns or a lack of procedural rights in a foreign criminal justice system' (*Martinez* 2015, 37). Its applicability is not mentioned in one leading Canadian text on extradition (Botting 2015), yet it is clearly valid in Australia despite few explicit references (*Adamas* 2013).

In *Perez* (2016b, 12), the court concluded the judge 'lack[ed] discretion to inquire into the conditions that might await a fugitive upon return to the requesting country'. In other words, the court decided that ruling on 'what is or is not legitimate' in the requesting country would potentially result in a 'grave insult' and 'would not be in keeping with the heightened principles of judicial modesty at play in an extradition proceeding' (*Nezirovic* 2013, 44–45). This view reinforces the importance of the rule of non-inquiry as a 'firmly established principle' of extradition law (*Mujagic* 2013, 55).

As a result, it is unlikely extraditees will receive judicial endorsement of arguments that raise the potential for violations of international human rights or domestic due process protections in the courts of requested nations. This is regardless of whether these claims are supported by compelling evidence documenting significant physical or mental health conditions or the likelihood of experiencing torture and other forms of targeted persecution. Consequently, the protection of individual rights remains largely a legal question for the requesting nation to rule on after surrender, regardless of a country's capacity or willingness to comply with international requirements (Warren and Palmer 2015). This reinforces the idea that extradition is part of a broader state-focused emphasis on transnational justice administration that favours respecting international comity and state sovereignty. This type of reasoning, and any resulting surrender decision, affirms patterns identified in extradition literature that demonstrate the power of the rule of non-inquiry to significantly limit the importance and relevance of individual protections (Aughterson 2005; Murchison 2007; Parry 2010; Quigley 1990), even if there are legitimate concerns over how justice or punishment is administered in requesting states (Bassiouni 1974, 2014; Pyle 2001; Rothe and Mullins 2010).

Conclusion

Despite the initial ruling that determined Assange was ineligible for extradition due to his mental health conditions and risk of suicide, and Savu's case, where it was decided he could submit additional information to the executive about potential mistreatment if surrendered to Romania because he was a Roma gypsy, each case described in this chapter ultimately found in favour of extradition and the rights of the requesting nation to seek the individual for trial or completion of a criminal sentence. The partial relief in these two cases is of limited consequence, as ultimately the decisions favouring each extraditee were overturned. These rulings uphold the rights and sovereign power of requesting nations to prosecute crimes (Arnell 2013, 2019; Mann and Warren 2018) through a transnational crime control philosophy (Boister 2003, 2015; Packer 1964; Roach 1999) that prioritises treaty compliance, political relationships and international cooperation between the requesting and requested nations over the rights of extraditees (Guzman 2002, 2005; Williams 1992). The limited relief in the Assange and Savu cases demonstrates that arguments by extraditees concerning their welfare can be recognised in court decisions considering extradition, yet are seldom granted legal weight. Therefore:

extradition necessarily entails an accommodation of conflicting interests. The desire to address international criminality and to adhere to international extradition agreements can be at odds with the human rights and welfare of requested persons. Simply, the cooperative and protective facets of the process cannot be wholly reconciled. (Arnell 2019, 371)

The next chapter explores similar concerns focusing on the conduct of the requesting and requested nations during the extradition process that could compromise fairness for the extraditee. The human rights issues emerging in these cases continue to highlight the need to consider reforms to the current extradition process.

Chapter 3

EXTRADITION IN PRACTICE: THE CONDUCT OF NATIONS

Introduction

The three cases described in this chapter highlight various concerns about specific conduct by the requesting and requested nations that could undermine the extraditee's individual rights. The high-profile case involving Kim Dotcom raises significant questions regarding the legality of search warrants executed by NZ Police to collect evidence to assist prosecutors in the US, and the operation of the double criminality rule. The quality of evidence against an extraditee was also raised in Hassan Diab's case, which examined the additional problem of when continued proceedings against the individual should cease. Finally, the case involving Daniel Snedden raises issues about the communication between nations when an extradition request has been made, and the application of the specialty principle, which stipulates an extraditee can only be prosecuted for the offences listed in the extradition request (Bassiouni 2014). This case also demonstrates how the political offence exception operates in the context of international crimes after protracted violent conflict and war. As with the cases in the previous chapter, there are few instances where judges supported the arguments raised by extraditees. The chapter will set out the key details of each case and illustrate problems when it comes to recognising the human rights of the extraditee during the surrender procedure.

Kim Dotcom, Police Action and Double Criminality

The Kim Dotcom case is a useful example that highlights the dilemmas facing police organisations asked to enforce a foreign extradition request while attempting to uphold domestic laws and individual rights protections that might differ from those in the requesting state. In this case, while US authorities held preliminary evidence that was sufficient to lay charges against Dotcom, Mathias Ortmann, Bram van der Kolk and several co-offenders, a successful prosecution required additional evidence that could only be collected by NZ Police under domestic search warrants. The legality of the NZ Police search and the issue of double criminality as judged by the NZ courts have been central to determining extraditability in this case.

As with Assange (see Chapter 2), Dotcom's activities stemmed from the creation of a popular online platform with global accessibility. Megaupload was an early precursor to many contemporary social media platforms that allowed users to share digital files indirectly through a system of active weblinks. Evidence from the US Federal Bureau of Investigations (FBI), which was supplemented by private surveillance from the US entertainment industry, discovered Megaupload was used to share unauthorised digital copies of films, television programs, computer software and other copyrighted works. Megaupload technically operated in Hong Kong, but leased servers in various countries. Dotcom and several colleagues named in the US indictment managed the business and site infrastructure in NZ. Despite being notified of millions of copyright breaches by a team of US investigators, site administrators developed a system of providing subscribers with active web links to conceal their failure to remove offending files uploaded by Megaupload users. This failure to enforce the takedown notices enabled subscribers to continue to access content that breached US intellectual property laws. The persistence of these alleged breaches arguably deprived legitimate copyright holders of an estimated $US500 million in revenues, although exact losses are impossible to calculate (*Ortmann and van der Kolk* 2023, para. 12). A US grand jury found sufficient evidence to proceed with five primary charges against Dotcom and other alleged co-offenders involving criminal copyright and related conspiracy offences. These offences were supplemented in a superseding indictment that listed several additional offences under US law, including money laundering and racketeering (Boister 2017b).

Legalities of the actions of NZ Police

In January 2012, NZ Police undertook the largest police raid in the country's history (Palmer and Warren 2013) in response to the US request to apprehend Dotcom, Ortmann, van der Kolk and two other named individuals and seize any 'evidence, fruits, and instrumentalities of the crimes being investigated' by the US (*Dotcom* 2012, para. 19). The NZ warrant authorising this search directly incorporated terms from the US extradition request and sought Dotcom and other key Megaupload staff but did not specify the material to be seized during the raid. Up to 150 terabytes of computer data, various digital devices, financial records and many luxury items that were considered to have been purchased from the profits generated by Megaupload were seized by NZ authorities and transferred to the US under the mutual legal assistance provisions of the UN *Convention against Transnational Organized Crime* (2000) (Boister 2017b, 201–4).

As with extradition law, mutual legal assistance provisions enable nations to transfer seized evidence during transnational criminal investigations. This process is also informed 'by international comity and the expectation that the assistance of police [in other jurisdictions] will be reciprocated when required' (Boister 2017b, 205). Most evidence in digitised form seized in the Dotcom case was cloned by the NZ Police and forwarded to the FBI against an express direction by the NZ Solicitor General (Palmer and Warren 2013, 109). As a result, most legal arguments associated with these proceedings emphasised the unlawful conduct of NZ Police in executing the warrant that sought to honour the US extradition request (Boister 2017b). Dotcom and his associates launched several complex legal actions in NZ to resist surrender and the seizure of their assets. The asset seizures ensure the financial dimensions of the case are entwined with the legal technicalities in defending extradition, given the monetary costs of extensive legal appeals lodged in the NZ courts since 2013.

The transfer of the evidence to US authorities was initially declared by NZ courts in 2013 to be unlawful as the warrant was unduly broad, which effectively labelled the search a 'fishing exercise' (Palmer and Warren 2013, 109). This decision was later overturned by the NZ Supreme Court and NZ Supreme Court of Appeal. These rulings emphasised information seized by NZ Police would simply supplement the extraterritorial evidence collected by US law enforcement agencies to compile the prosecution case and take down Megaupload (Boister 2017b, 197–98).

This key issue demonstrates the power of international comity in shaping distinct legal approaches that favour honouring an extradition request. Despite acknowledging law enforcement conduct in response to an extradition request must comply with requirements that apply to any pretrial or criminal proceedings conducted in NZ under the *Bill of Rights Act* (1990) (*Dotcom* 2014, paras. 50–53), many anomalies in the content and execution of the procedure in NZ were found to be not 'so radical as to consider the warrant a nullity' (Boister 2017b, 207). In other words, the appeal courts took a broad view to upholding the legal validity of the NZ warrant. Thus, even though the form of the US request raised several questions about the validity of the warrant and its subsequent execution by NZ Police, its practical effect caused no 'significant prejudice' to Dotcom or anyone affiliated with Megaupload (Boister 2017b, 209). While acknowledging the warrant and police conduct in NZ was effectively a blanket search of

Dotcom's premises, its impact in light of more specific criteria under the NZ *Bill of Rights Act* (1990) could be excused because the request was systematic, made in good faith and could be readily interpreted as relevant to the US case against Megaupload. That this broader perspective countered a narrower view expressed in earlier appeals against the legality of the search and seizure under NZ law highlights the technical difficulties in ensuring the content of extradition requests matches the domestic laws of both the requesting and the requested states.

Double criminality

Double or dual criminality is considered a universal principle of extradition law. However, its application in domestic extradition cases can vary considerably (Williams 1991). This principle requires extradition courts to consider whether the offences listed in a request match those listed in the criminal laws of a requested state. The overall objective of ensuring a matching offence in the state receiving an extradition request is to prevent the surrender and punishment of extraditees 'for conduct considered contrary to the requested state's own [...] notions of criminal justice' (Dugard and Van den Wyngaert 1998, 188). As a report cited by the NZ High Court explains, double criminality:

> helps to protect the alleged offender's basic human rights, given that the person is threatened with removal from the safety of a state where he or she has committed no offence. (*Ortmann* 2018, para. 79)

Consideration of double criminality requires extradition courts to undertake a comparative examination of the legal requirements for proving the offence under its own laws, in light of those listed in the extradition request. An exact match of the laws in each jurisdiction is not required. Rather, double criminality will be satisfied if the extradition treaty contains a list of agreed offences, or if the offences are functionally equivalent to existing crimes in the laws of the requested nation (Williams 1991). Many treaties and domestic extradition laws will specify a broad range of offences that are subject to a minimum duration of imprisonment in the state receiving the request, known as the eliminative approach. For instance, the NZ *Extradition Act* (1999) specifies the offence must be punishable under NZ law where the 'maximum penalty is imprisonment for not less than 12 months' (*Ortmann* 2018, para. 329). This phrasing sidesteps a direct comparison of the content of differing laws under what is termed an enumerative approach (Boister 2017b), which specifically lists the extraditable offences in a treaty or domestic extradition legislation (*Ortmann* 2018, para. 50).

Applying the double criminality test under an enumerative approach is extremely complex and requires examining whether the facts and laws listed in the extradition request would meet a legal threshold for laying equivalent charges in the receiving state (Boister 2017b). An additional case considered by the NZ High Court (*Ortmann* 2018) that was appealed to the Supreme Court (*Ortmann* 2020) considered whether NZ laws contained equivalent provisions to US offences involving conspiracy to commit racketeering, obtaining money through wire fraud, conspiracy to commit money laundering and a series of less serious charges involving the unlawful distribution of specific copyrighted works and conspiracy to infringe copyright on a commercial scale. Each of these offences was listed in the request against Dotcom and his associates. The double criminality test required NZ courts to examine whether equivalent crimes were listed in the terms of the *Treaty on Extradition between New Zealand and the United States of America* (1970), the NZ *Crimes Act* (1961), the NZ *Extradition Act* (1999) and the NZ *Copyright Act* (1994).

Two key rulings examined the relevant sections of each NZ law in light of the 'essential conduct' considered necessary to establish the offences listed in the US request (*Ortmann* 2018, para. 133). For example, when determining the essential conduct of the copyright offences, both the NZ High Court and the NZ Supreme Court examined whether Megaupload staff and developers knew their failure to remove files uploaded by site users that were identified by US authorities in a takedown notice would establish the intention of Dotcom and his associates to commit an offence under equivalent NZ criminal copyright provisions (*Ortmann* 2020, para. 388). In finding this was the case based on evidence listed in the US extradition request, the NZ High Court stated:

> the essential conduct alleged is that the appellants would receive a digital file from users of Megaupload, convert and store the file on servers leased for that purpose and, via a URL link, enable users access to that file which they could then share with other users (albeit not on a Megaupload site) for the purpose of enabling others to access that content. (*Ortmann* 2018, para. 187)

Arguments by Dotcom and associates suggested there was no breach of NZ law because Megaupload only shared a URL linking to the file, rather than the file itself, once a takedown notice was received. However, this argument was rejected due to decisions by Megaupload staff to remove some files, while issuing new URLs for files that were popular among users. This complex assessment required NZ courts to transpose the facts of the case onto existing offences in NZ law. The result was Dotcom, Ortmann, van der Kolk and two others were found eligible for extradition to the US to face all charges bar a single charge of conspiracy to commit money laundering, which had no equivalent offence under NZ law (*Ortmann* 2021).

Subsequent developments

In June 2023, Ortmann and van der Kolk were sentenced under NZ law to just over two and a half years imprisonment after pleading guilty to participating in an organised criminal group, conspiring to cause loss by deception and conspiring to dishonestly obtain documents. This decision emerged after US authorities agreed to suspend all extradition and related criminal proceedings against them in exchange for their pleas of guilty, their conviction and sentencing under NZ laws and their agreement to cooperate in any future US proceedings against Megaupload (*Ortmann and van der Kolk* 2023, para. 3). Dotcom publicly empathised with this decision, though at the time of writing continues to question the summary of facts against Ortmann and van der Kolk that informed their guilty pleas. A decision on Dotcom's surrender rests with the NZ Minister of Justice after over a decade of extensive judicial scrutiny.

Hassan Diab, Evidence and Continued Proceedings

In most circumstances, individuals facing extradition are unable to submit evidence which directly contradicts the facts of the case presented by the requesting nation. This is known as the rule of non-contradiction (Semmelman 1999), which means 'evidence that *contradicts* or *controverts* the existence of probable cause is inadmissible, including evidence establishing a defense or exonerating the accused' (*Luna-Ruiz* 2014, 36, emphasis in original). However, the non-contradiction rule can be overly restrictive on a person wishing to challenge extradition (Angelson 2009).

The operation and inconsistency of this rule is illustrated by the Hassan Diab case. Diab was born in Lebanon in 1953, received a PhD in sociology and became a Canadian citizen in 2006. When France sent an extradition request to Canada in 2008, Diab held positions at Carleton University and the University of Ottawa and had no prior criminal record. The extradition request sought Diab for his alleged role in a bombing outside a synagogue in Paris in October 1980, which resulted in four counts of murder, 40 counts of attempted murder and various charges relating to the destruction of property. The bombing was described as 'an act of terrorism, a hate crime' (*Diab* 2009, 6).

Diab was arrested by Canadian authorities in November 2008 and granted bail in March 2009 (*Diab* 2009). This case provides an important example of the evidentiary limitations during extradition hearings and the continued willingness of the requesting country to pursue an extraditee despite what may appear to be a finalisation of the case.

Questions about evidence

In 2009 and 2010, Diab's common law spouse, Rania Tfaily, raised concerns about an order issued in Canada requiring her home and work computers to be seized as a result of search warrants issued under the *Mutual Legal Assistance in Criminal Matters Act* (1985) and a partial order that would send electronic images of the hard drives of these devices to France (*Tfaily* 2009, 2010). While leave to appeal the partial sending order was granted (*Tfaily* 2009), the appeal against the seizure of her computers failed because there was evidence Diab may have been communicating via email with other members of a terrorist organisation using Tfaily's computer (*Tfaily* 2010).

These concerns about evidence were examined further in *Diab* (2010), where a court ruled on the admissibility of evidence from handwriting experts. A report from Anne Biscotti, a French handwriting expert, stated Diab was the likely author of a guest registration card at a hotel near the site of the bombing in Paris. This supported the inference from other evidence that whoever filled in the registration card was responsible for planting the bomb. Diab sought to introduce evidence from experts who believed Biscotti's conclusions were unreliable and flawed, but if this evidence was used it would transform the extradition proceedings into a criminal trial. The judge determined that an extradition court is not allowed to weigh the 'ultimate reliability' of any evidence as this is 'the responsibility of the finder of fact' during prosecution (*Diab* 2010, para. 14). However, despite this finding, evidence from both Biscotti and Diab's experts was allowed in the Canadian extradition hearing, seemingly in opposition to the rule of non-contradiction.

In June 2011, a Canadian magistrate found Diab eligible for surrender, while dismissing four of the five pieces of evidence submitted on behalf of France because they were considered insufficient to justify extradition (*Diab* 2011). However, an analysis of handwriting that linked Diab to the suspected bomber could not be completely rejected as unreliable. An argument that surrender would be unjust, oppressive and violate section 7 of the *Canadian Charter* (1982), which protects the life, liberty and security of the person, was dismissed despite Diab's concern the extradition request relied on unsourced intelligence and evidence potentially obtained via torture.

This ruling led the Canadian executive to sign Diab's extradition order in April 2012.

On appeal, Diab argued the magistrate's ruling on the reliability of the admissible evidence was too narrow and questioned the method for conducting the handwriting analysis (*Diab* 2014a). Diab also argued the Minister of Justice 'misunderstood his submissions, considered irrelevant factors and misapplied the law to reach an unreasonable conclusion' during the executive decision-making phase (*Diab* 2014a, para. 9). Similar to the result in *Diab* (2010), the court found the magistrate had the power to determine the reliability of evidence presented in the French extradition request and related hearings. Therefore, the magistrate's decision was not considered an error. It was also found the minister had correctly concluded that 'France does not condone the use of torture-derived evidence', and any concerns Diab might have about the use of such evidence 'can be addressed through appropriate mechanisms' when a criminal trial commences in France (*Diab* 2014a, para. 272).

Not the place for arguments about evidence

Extradition cases have highly restrictive approaches to evidence that tend to favour the requesting state (Andreas and Nadelmann 2006; Magnuson 2012; Pyle 2001). Unusually, Diab was given permission to submit contradictory handwriting analysis, although he was found to be eligible for extradition. This highlights that most concerns about evidence are 'submission[s] properly made at a trial, not in an extradition hearing' (*Doak* 2013, para. 29).

Even when evidence is circumstantial or contradictory, only a 'limited weighing exercise' is required by an extradition court to determine whether an 'inference in favour of the [requesting nation] is reasonable' (*Viscomi* 2015, para. 20). This means the evidence must not be:

> manifestly unreliable. It may not be enough to obtain a conviction, but that is not the test. As long as there is some evidence available for trial, and it is not manifestly unreliable, the person sought will be committed for extradition. It is not for the extradition judge to determine the strength or weakness of the evidence beyond determining whether it is manifestly unreliable. (*Le* 2014, para. 26)

The Diab case, and others like it, support the extradition literature which consistently emphasises high evidentiary thresholds must be met to successfully argue against extradition (Arnell 2013, 2018; Parry 2010). This means only a limited number of cases acknowledge evidentiary arguments involving human rights issues that are raised by extraditees.

Continued proceedings

After a final unsuccessful appeal (*Diab* 2014b), according to a media report by Daigle and Cochrane (2018), Diab was extradited to France in 2014 and spent more than three years in prison despite never being formally charged. Diab was released in January 2018 after a French court found the evidence was insufficient to continue to trial and that he may have been in Lebanon at the time of the bombing. At this time, it was also revealed that prior to the extradition request, in May 2007, France was aware of, but failed to disclose to Canada, fingerprint evidence and other forensic analysis that placed further doubt on Diab's involvement in the bombing (Cochrane and Laventure 2018). Diab ultimately returned to Canada after being surrendered to France on insufficient and unreliable evidence.

In 2019, an independent review of Diab's extradition was conducted by Murray Segal, a former Deputy Attorney General of Ontario. This review found that legal counsel working on behalf of the Canadian Department of Justice 'acted in a manner that was ethical and consistent' and behaved 'properly in vigorously advancing France's case' (Segal 2019, 8). However, it was also noted that:

> With the benefit of hindsight, it is apparent that counsel presenting the case for extradition could have entertained different approaches to the complex issues of this case, which might have resulted in more expedient and less hotly contested proceedings. Going forward, the Department of Justice should consider adopting policies and procedures that promote both fairness and efficiencies in extradition proceedings – *even when these procedures are not strictly required by the law.* (Segal 2019, 8, emphasis added)

In January 2020, Diab and his family sued the Canadian federal government for $90 million in damages (Haig 2020). However, this claim was discontinued in August 2023 (CNW 2023). Meanwhile, France appealed the January 2018 decision to dismiss the trial and Diab was convicted and sentenced to life imprisonment *in absentia* in April 2023 (Al Jazeera 2023). While it is currently unclear whether France will send a second request to Canada seeking Diab's extradition to serve the sentence, this can theoretically occur if a new application with appropriate detail is provided. Unlike the rule of double jeopardy which prevents repeated criminal trials in domestic courts, the absence of limits on the number of extradition requests can lead to potential abuse of process (Blakesley 1980).

Daniel Snedden, Communication and the Political Offence Exception

Daniel Snedden, also known as Dragan Vasiljkovic and Captain Dragan, was involved in a 'lengthy and complex [extradition case] [...] in no small way due to Mr Snedden's challenges to various stages of the process' (*Snedden* 2014, para. 2). This case raised concerns about the right an extraditee has to be involved in or view the communications occurring between the requesting and requested nations, which has specific implications if one nation raises issues about the protection of the individual. Snedden was sought for international war crimes for alleged activities in the former Yugoslavia, which adds further complexity to the case given the potential for people of Serbian origin to receive unfair trials in the aftermath of this conflict (Hagan and Ivković 2006). The case also highlights the role of universal jurisdiction and the prospective operation of the political offence exception under extradition procedure and international criminal law.

Snedden was born in the former Yugoslavia in 1954, arrived in Australia in 1969 and obtained Australian citizenship in 1975. He returned to Yugoslavia in 1990 and became the commander of a special unit of the Serbian Paramilitary Troops, which at the time was in armed conflict with the army of the Republic of Croatia. In 1991 and 1993, Snedden was alleged to have been involved in two offences against prisoners of war after soldiers under his command tortured and killed members of the Croatian army and police. He was also accused of one offence against civilians who were wounded and killed when buildings were damaged during a military attack. Snedden returned to Australia after the conflict and Croatia issued an extradition request in February 2006, which generated nine years of legal appeals in the Australian courts (*Vasiljkovic* 2006a, 2006b, 2010, 2011; *Snedden* 2007, 2009a, 2009b, 2010, 2013, 2014).

Communication about the specialty principle

A primary feature of the Snedden case is whether he had a clear right to access and legally challenge communications between Australia and Croatia about the operation of the specialty principle. As a central rule of extradition, the specialty principle aims to provide a guarantee from the requesting state that the extraditee will only be tried for the offences listed in the extradition request (Abbell 2010; Aughterson 2005; Bassiouni 2014). However, specialty is not applied as a consistent norm of customary international law and the legal status of this test remains ill-defined (Forstein 2015). This means its operation is likely to vary. Importantly, the Snedden case demonstrates the limited active role an extraditee has during the surrender process. Extraditees do not have a right to examine all communications between the nations involved, even if these might reveal potential rights violations and concerns the requested nation may have about surrender.

In September 2011, Croatia provided Australia with an assurance under the specialty principle that Snedden would not be charged with additional offences. Then, in November 2012, the Australian Minister for Justice determined Snedden should be surrendered. In appealing this decision, Snedden claimed he had been denied procedural fairness because he was not given the opportunity to respond to material sent and received by Australia, which included the assurance of specialty from Croatia. However, the Minister for Justice argued:

> that while procedural fairness required him to put Mr Snedden's claims to the Croatian authorities because Croatia is the extradition country, he was not obliged to put Croatia's response to Mr Snedden because no new considerations or matters were raised in the response. (*Snedden* 2013, para. 35)

The court disagreed and determined that even if the Croatian response raised no new considerations, any new information was *potentially* relevant to Snedden's extradition challenge. As such, procedural fairness required Snedden be given the opportunity to examine Croatia's response and make further submissions if needed. The court surmised that:

> Snedden was entitled to know that Australia had concerns about whether additional charges may be brought against him and had sought further clarification from Croatia after the specialty assurance was received. (*Snedden* 2013, para. 45)

The matter was remitted to the Minister of Justice for redetermination, although Snedden appealed this order to obtain a complete and finalised denial of extradition (*Snedden* 2014). Again, the Minister of Justice argued there is 'no absolute obligation' to provide an extraditee with the opportunity to reply directly to the requesting country's submissions and the information from Croatia was 'purely responsive' to Australia's enquiries (*Snedden* 2014, para. 89–90).

The court found Snedden was given ample opportunity to present appropriate and relevant information during the original submission phase. He had also not specifically asked to respond to Croatia's new submissions and was not operating under an assumption that he had an automatic right of reply to each element of Croatia's case. The court stated there was 'no practical unfairness' and 'no new information within the Croatian response that was adverse, credible, relevant and significant such that procedural fairness required the minister to provide that information' (*Snedden* 2014, para. 222). This means an extraditee is not entitled to receive or challenge every communication between states to be ensured a fair extradition hearing. Although Snedden argued the evidence showed concern about the 'validity or genuineness of the specialty assurance', the court rejected this argument because the communication between Australia and Croatia 'does not support such an inference', but instead highlighted a 'process of clarification and confirmation about the assurance received' (*Snedden* 2014, para. 231).

According to media reports by Vladisavljevic (2018, 2019), Snedden was extradited to Croatia in July 2015 and sentenced to a 15-year imprisonment term in September 2017, with consideration given to previous time spent in both Australian and Croatian detention. The sentence was reduced to a 13-year and six-month term in July 2018. Requests for early release were denied in November 2018 and September 2019 because Snedden remained unapologetic. A news item by Magnay et al. (2020) indicated Snedden was released from prison in March 2020 and returned to Serbia where he ventured into a career in politics. He has been banned from entering any EU country for 20 years and Australian authorities were considering revoking his Australian passport and residency rights. Ultimately, the prosecution and conviction were found not to have violated the specialty principle.

The political offence exception and international crime

The application of the political offence exception to alleged breaches of international criminal law adds further complexity to the Snedden case. The political offence exception enables a state to refuse an extradition request if the alleged conduct was a political act or surrender is for political purposes (Dugard and Van den Wyngaert 1998). Historically, this exception sought to ensure an extraditee received a fair trial or was not persecuted for holding beliefs that were contrary to the political climate in the requesting state (Petersen 1992). However, the notion of a political offence is ill-defined (Sicalides 1989, 1299) and this element of extradition law is considered to be of declining importance (Griffith and Harris 2005, 43–44). Most scholarly research on the political offence exception in the context of international crime is decades old (see Garcia-Mora 1962; Green 1962; Neumann 1951) and significantly predates recent developments in international criminal law that include the establishment of specialist tribunals in the former Yugoslavia and Rwanda and the formation of the International Criminal Court to prosecute alleged war crimes, crimes against humanity and genocide.

The alleged political motivation behind Croatia's request to extradite Snedden was raised in communications between Australian and Croatian authorities. Snedden argued his trial would be prejudiced due to his political opinions and nationality because he supported a core idea that was behind the conflict in the former Yugoslavia that 'Krajina Serbs have a right to return to their homeland and are entitled to an independent state' (*Snedden* 2009b, para. 53). While it is rare for the political offence exception to be the basis for refusing a properly drafted extradition request (Bassiouni 1984, 574), the Full Court of the Federal Court of Australia accepted that Snedden's Serbian background could expose him to prejudice if a criminal trial proceeded in Croatia (*Snedden* 2009b). Research supports this concern among Serbs facing charges for international crimes associated with the conflict (Hagan and Ivkovic 2006). However, this argument was overturned by the High Court of Australia, which upheld Snedden's eligibility for extradition because any suggestion of possible prejudice based on his political opinions or nationality rested on evidence that was 'too feeble' (*Snedden* 2010a, para. 102). This outcome highlights the limited ability of extraditees to successfully challenge extradition requests given the degree of judicial deference towards upholding the relationship between the requesting and requested nations.

It is particularly noteworthy that extradition might be largely irrelevant in cases involving allegations of international crime. This is because war crimes, crimes against humanity and genocide are subject to universal jurisdiction, a form of extraterritorial jurisdiction that enables any nation to assert legal authority over an allegation of international crime regardless of the location of the offending (Abelson 2009; Bassiouni 1974, 2014; Blakesley 1982, 1984, 2008; Harvard Research 1935; Ireland-Piper 2012). While there might be clear evidentiary problems in cases of this nature, the existence of universal jurisdiction potentially removes the need for extradition in these situations.

Conclusion

The cases presented in this chapter demonstrate further legal and procedural challenges associated with the current law of extradition. They reinforce the high degree of legal technicality associated with cases involving suspected large-scale cyber offences, terrorism and war crimes, all of which are of significant transnational and international concern. They also highlight difficulties in applying technical rules, including double criminality and evidentiary requirements under the non-contradiction guideline, which compromise the ability of prospective extraditees to lodge meaningful legal challenges to surrender that protect their rights. The next chapter builds on the issues outlined in this chapter and Chapter 2 to highlight potential pathways for reforming the laws of extradition, given the clear tendency for domestic courts to uphold comity between nations, while limiting the human rights grounds individual extraditees can legitimately raise when challenging an extradition request.

Chapter 4

THE NEED FOR REFORM

Introduction

The cases examined in this book illustrate that individual protections during the extradition process emerge in two ways. The first involves human rights protected under international laws, such as the CAT and related treaties. The second is through due process rights in national legal systems applied in individual cases, which are subject to the rule of non-inquiry. Human rights protected under international law emerge occasionally in the cases presented in Chapters 2 and 3. However, high evidentiary standards are commonly needed to establish viable human rights arguments under domestic extradition laws (Arnell 2013; Cullen and Burgess 2015; Parry 2010). Due process or procedural concerns in the administration of justice in requesting states appear more common, yet remain equally difficult to challenge in extradition courts (Dugard and Van den Wyngaert 1998). Both executive and judicial approaches to extradition must consider how requesting states meet basic international and domestic human rights standards, as 'obligations to protect individuals should not end at our borders' (Bifani 1993, 660). This is despite some experts arguing extradition should become a purely administrative process by eroding its substantive and procedural elements, including the need for the requesting state to provide evidence to support a claim for surrender (Boister 2017a).

This chapter examines core human rights and due process issues that commonly emerge in extradition cases. It links the existence of these protective rights to significant elements of criminal justice administration, while positing why these arguments are rarely successful in legal challenges to an extradition request. The chapter then explores the importance of a defendant-centred approach to help clarify the status of individual rights in extradition law (Gless 2013) and proposes some specific reforms to the current extradition procedure. Broader implications for the potential universalisation of contemporary criminal law are then discussed.

Rights in Extradition Law

This section summarises key individual rights claims which can arise during the extradition process, many of which are demonstrated in the cases examined in this book, and aligns them with core elements of the criminal justice process. This includes discussion of prominent international human rights protections, vulnerabilities based on an extraditee's age and health, formal rules relating to bail, access to legal representation, the conduct of fair trials, issues relating to evidence and sentencing, and the legal tensions associated with judicial and executive decision-making.

International law protections

International human rights protections usually require incorporation into domestic legal systems to be given formal recognition by extradition courts or executive decisions. For example, despite claims in the Perez case of potential exposure to torture that contravened the CAT, the court found it lacked the discretion to examine the conditions of detention in a foreign country. This result highlights the unwillingness of US courts to recognise the significance of international human rights claims when examining the criminal justice processes in requesting states.

The tension between domestic and international human rights requirements appears to stem from the failure to integrate international protections within domestic criminal justice frameworks. Any human rights grounds specified in international treaties are not always readily translatable or enforceable in domestic criminal courts. Hence, the protective elements of international human rights claims have been subject to high evidentiary thresholds that are established on a case-by-case basis in domestic extradition courts (Cullen and Burgess 2015). This means any potential international human rights violation must be specific to the extraditee, rather than simply a general pattern associated with a requesting state's criminal justice processes, such as routine misconduct that results in unfair trials or institutional tolerance of substandard prison conditions. Arguments establishing prospective human rights violations specific to the extraditee are extremely difficult to prove and will always involve a degree of speculation. Proof of customary or regular human rights violations in administering justice in requesting states appears insufficient to bar extradition (Arnell 2013; Parry 2010).

Status of the extraditee

Extradition can be barred under most transnational crime control treaties, including the *Budapest Convention* (2001) (Clough 2014), where evidence establishes a likelihood the extraditee will face persecution due to their race, sex, religion, nationality, ethnic origins or political opinions (Dugard and Van den Wyngaert 1998; Griffith and Harris 2005). However, the acceptance of these terms varies among signatory nations (Roberg 2007; Rogoff 1980) given national courts have discretion to determine extraditability relating to any of these grounds. This discretion involves considering whether the request discloses any motives for the extraditee's prosecution in the requesting state. Here, it seems the underlying rationale for making the request will be assumed by the nature of the offence and any accompanying evidentiary details, which might stem from questionable aspects of law enforcement or surveillance activity in both the requesting and requested states (Rogers 2023).

Extradition courts have a difficult responsibility when determining the underlying motives for any extradition request. For example, this obligation can modify the operation of the political offence exception, which is an important historic protection against extradition. However, confining consideration of the likelihood of persecution to an extraditee's race, sex, religion, nationality, ethnic origins or political opinions has the potential to undermine scrutiny of the political nature of certain criminal charges, which rests at the philosophical core of the political offence exception. There are clear political imperatives behind the charges of espionage against Assange and the terrorism allegations involving Diab which can compromise a fair trial in the requesting states. Current laws focusing on the likelihood of prejudice based on the extraditee's personal status fail to consider how such offences are, in fact, inherently political (Petersen 1992).

Interestingly, there is also no specific bar on extradition due to a person's age or other personal infirmities (Cullen and Burgess 2015, 237). This means concerns over how Assange's medical diagnosis will be managed in the US are dealt with through political assurances, rather than concrete human rights protections that recognise any medical care he is receiving in the UK is likely to be implemented through different clinical standards if he is surrendered. As the McKinnon case illustrates (see Chapter 1), the executive can override judicial rulings that do not give adequate weight to the impact of surrender on an extraditee's physical or mental health, particularly after protracted extradition proceedings or where the offending conduct emanated from outside the requesting state, which is common in many allegations of transnational cyber offending (Mann et al. 2018). However, questions involving age and infirmity have also been prominent since the end of World War II, where it has often taken decades for suspects to be identified for their involvement in serious international crimes, which then leads to protracted legal appeals to determine their extraditability. One example is the case of Charles Zentai, which involved several appeals to decide whether a man aged

88 years should be extradited from Australia to Hungary to face charges relating to his involvement in alleged war crimes dating back to 1944 (*Zentai* 2012). While there is a clear need to ensure justice is administered for such serious historic conduct, the welfare of ageing and infirm extraditees can be impacted by their removal from established medical and family supports. The High Court of Australia eventually blocked Zentai's extradition as war crimes were not an offence under Hungarian law at the time of the alleged conduct (*Zentai* 2012). Zentai died in Perth, Australia, in December 2017 without facing trial (Butterly 2017). As with the Snedden case, these allegations could possibly have led to a criminal trial in Australia under the principles of universal jurisdiction that apply to international crimes.

The citizenship status of the extraditee can also have varied impacts in extradition cases. Jurisdictions adopting civil law approaches to criminal procedure commonly prevent the extradition of their nationals (Blakesley 2008; Plachta 1999). This rule has a protective rationale based on the historic idea that a non-national of the requesting state was more likely to experience an unfair trial (Baronia 2021). However, this rule does not encapsulate scenarios such as the Assange case, where the state receiving the request is required to decide on the extraditability of a national from a third country that is not party to the extradition treaty. Third-party nationals and nationals with limited connection to either the requesting or requested state create several practical dilemmas for extradition courts as no specific human rights or due process rules directly address their status. This problem often arises where the alleged criminal conduct in the extradition request occurs remotely or extraterritorially.

The increased global movement of people no longer ensures an extraditee will have a physical, national or cultural attachment to either the requesting or requested states, where disparate conceptions of rights and the scope of criminal law are likely. This disjuncture is directly tied to territorial jurisdiction that informs both extradition and criminal law. The rule governing the non-extradition of nationals can offer some protection for citizens in certain jurisdictions, yet at the same time can subvert the ideals of justice promoted by the extradition process.

Bail and legal representation

The availability of bail will vary under different national extradition laws. Australia has a legal presumption against bail unless the extraditee can establish special circumstances to justify remaining in the community while extraditability is being determined. This differs slightly from laws governing bail in domestic criminal cases because as a fugitive from the requesting state, an extraditee is more likely to be considered a flight risk (*Tsvetnenko* 2019). This means bail is generally refused even if an extraditee offers to surrender their passport, submit to electronic tagging or agrees to any other court-imposed conditions (see Kennedy and Warren 2022).

Assange's decision to enter the Ecuadorian Embassy was a breach of bail conditions relating to the Swedish EAW (*Assange* 2019a). By contrast, bail conditions set for Dotcom have not been breached for over a decade. Such variations in pre-surrender detention result from the failure of extradition treaties to specify clear minimum standards for the right to bail. Pre-extradition detention is commonly dealt with through sentencing discounts for time served if a person is surrendered to and convicted in the requesting state.

Access to legal representation is a fundamental due process right that is assumed to be available in extradition cases. This question has not been argued in any cases documented in this book. However, according to one US ruling, the lack of publicly funded legal assistance in the US state of Virginia was considered insufficient to block extradition (Dugard and Van den Wyngaert 1998, 203). This ruling suggests courts considering extradition requests should have some capacity to examine the availability of appropriate legal representation in the requesting state.

Fair trial and evidence

The rule of non-inquiry reinforces a presumption that any criminal trial in the requesting state will be conducted fairly and consistently with the due process requirements of the state receiving the request. Paradoxically, such an assessment does not examine what is likely to occur in the requesting state. Rather, the inquiry is conducted notionally, or by proxy, based on standards in the requested state. This process reinforces the nature of extradition as an agreement or contract between states, with minimal scope for extradition courts to scrutinise the administration of justice in nations issuing requests. This is concerning due to some disturbing anecdotes by US prosecutors suggesting extraditees who delay criminal trials by asserting their rights to challenge a request deserve harsher treatment in criminal trials upon surrender (Botting 2005, 7).

Perhaps the most significant due process issue relates to the quality and admissibility of evidence. Extradition hearings are analogous to preliminary hearings that determine the sufficiency of evidence in support of criminal charges. These processes enable suspects to present limited evidence outlining their arguments challenging the request or charge. However, as demonstrated in the Diab and Dotcom cases, questions regarding both the reliability and admissibility of evidence to support a request, and in the former case an *in absentia* conviction, raise doubts regarding the legal merits behind a decision to extradite.

This issue is prominent in many cases involving transnational digital surveillance. The Assange and Dotcom cases highlight how digital data readily transcends national conceptions of territorial sovereignty and is increasingly viewed as un-territorial (Daskal 2015, 2017). This can lead to unmonitored surveillance practices by law enforcement agencies in both the requesting and requested nations (Rogers 2023), which can later be deemed inadmissible in both countries. However, questions on the admissibility of evidence are not commonly examined in extradition hearings. The only questions regarding evidence relevant to the Dotcom case related to the information taken by NZ Police that was later transferred to US authorities. There was no judicial consideration of the evidence listed by the US in the record of the case, or its potential admissibility in either a US or NZ court. This is despite concerns that the collaborative surveillance activities of NZ and US intelligence agencies were technically unlawful in NZ (Rogers 2023).

A similar problem emerges with the physical evidence used in the Diab case. Here, Canadian extradition courts invoked an exception to allow scrutiny of handwriting evidence that was central to the French request. The Canadian courts indicated this evidence had dubious reliability, though this was insufficient to block Diab's surrender and resulted in his *in absentia* conviction in subsequent French criminal proceedings in 2023. While evidentiary challenges of this nature are extremely rare, they can reinforce the protective nature of extradition law in line with accepted due process standards in the requested nation.

Rather than attempting to address this concern, there is an increasing tendency for extradition treaties to streamline evidentiary procedures. For example, the US treaty with Canada enables a US request to be granted by Canada solely with evidence listed in the record of the case that accompanies the extradition petition. While similar provisions are evident in many US extradition treaties (Palmer and Warren 2013), the same requirement is not permitted for many nations issuing requests to the US, including Canada and NZ. This imbalance can promote delays to surrender procedures considered by US extradition courts, while simultaneously promoting a fast-tracked process of surrender to the US because its claims are based on unsworn evidence that is largely unchallengeable. Botting (2005) points to the imbalance created by these treaty arrangements by referring to cases where Canada has ordered the surrender of an extraditee based on unsworn evidence that lacks credibility, involves statements classifiable as hearsay evidence or has resulted in the wrong person being surrendered.

Sentencing

Parity and proportionality are central to domestic sentencing laws. However, these issues are seldom examined in extradition cases. The *Söering* (1989) decision indirectly sets a key precedent regarding parity because the ECtHR found exposure to the death penalty itself is not a clear basis for preventing extradition. Rather, the human rights bar related to Söering's potential exposure to the death row phenomenon, which involves the experience of anxiety the death penalty is likely to cause an extraditee pending execution (Dugard and Van den Wyngaert 1998; *Söering* 1989). A shift towards non-extraditability in cases where the death penalty can be imposed appears to have evolved into a standard element of contemporary extradition law (Dugard and Van den Wyngaert 1998). However, this shift is driven largely by executive decision-making when extradition treaties are formulated or through the provision of assurances, rather than judicial rulings examining the human rights impacts of sentencing practices in requesting nations.

The eliminative approach raised in the Dotcom case is one way extradition treaties can sidestep the requirement for judicial consideration of sentencing parity and proportionality. This approach involves setting a minimum sentencing cap to determine whether an offence is extraditable. While notionally designed to remove the complexity of the double criminality test, which is associated with the enumerative approach of listing specific types of offences within extradition treaties, the Dotcom case illustrates the eliminative approach will not necessarily achieve this aim. Notably, the convictions of Ortmann and van der Kolk indicate the considerable sentencing disparities between NZ and the US for equivalent offences.

The eliminative approach to double criminality can result in a very low minimum sentencing cap of imprisonment for up to one year for extraditable offences. This raises concerns about the potentially disproportionate nature of surrender for less serious offences. For example, in the Savu case, the extraditee was convicted *in absentia* for fraud and forgery and sentenced to a term of imprisonment of five years and six months. Arguably, the severity of the offence and penalty are quite low, raising questions about whether it is oppressive or disproportionate to extradite, even if it is in the requesting state's interests to prosecute or ensure a convicted person serves a sentence.

The issue of cumulative sentencing emerges in the Assange and Dotcom cases, both of whom face over 150 years in prison if convicted on all charges listed in their respective extradition requests. Currently, extradition law offers no guidance on the relative merits of cumulative or concurrent sentencing, even though arguments from *Söering* (1989) about the psychological impact of the death penalty could readily be applied to a sentence of life imprisonment, or longer, in a foreign jurisdiction. Chapter 1 demonstrates judicial authorities remain reluctant to expand the principle identified in *Söering* (1989) to non-capital offences or to examine sentencing practices more generally due to the rule of non-inquiry.

Domestic decision-making bodies

While judicial and executive roles in extradition proceedings are relatively clear, domestic approaches to the authority of each varies. For example, reforms to Canadian extradition law introduced in 1999 expanded the powers of the executive while raising questions over the purpose of the judicial function (Botting 2005, xix). By contrast, the EAW procedure, which aims to streamline extradition among the EU Member States, is underpinned by the mutual recognition of judicial decisions. As such, a ruling from a 'judicial authority in one member state receive(s) full and direct effect throughout the EU' (Efrat and Newman 2020, 585). These variations have a profound impact on how international human rights and domestic due process claims are incorporated into extradition law by compromising the development of clear and consistent judicial processes that can protect extraditees.

The cases examined in this book and throughout the extradition literature highlight judicial reluctance to recognise compelling arguments that the surrender of extraditees can compromise their personal well-being. For example, Perez was extradited despite compelling humanitarian and personal grounds that could justify waiving the rule of non-inquiry (*Perez* 2016b). Baronia (2021) identified a similar problem associated with the willingness of US courts to uphold extradition requests despite clear evidence of potential persecution in states with poor adherence to the requirements of the CAT. While such judicial decisions can be overridden by executive action, as in McKinnon's case (Mann et al. 2018), discretionary executive oversight is not accountable in the same way as independent judicial review and does not lead to the development of clear human rights precedents that inform and refine the evolution of extradition law.

Towards a Defendant-Centred Approach

In proposing the following reforms, the objective is to emphasise the centrality of 'space' in criminal justice administration, rather than 'place' or the specific territorial location that currently underpins jurisdictional claims under both extradition and criminal law (Zumbansen 2012, 334). Currently, the centrality of territorial sovereignty unnecessarily politicises the role of human rights as a protective element of extradition law. It is necessary to move beyond this political dimension to ensure the meaningful recognition of human rights claims by acknowledging extradition rulings are 'not limited to national criminal justice systems' (Gless 2013, 108), but are simply administered domestically to facilitate these processes where clearer and more coherent approaches to transnational justice administration have yet to develop or mature. The laws of extradition in national systems were initially established to incorporate transnational and global justice values that have changed markedly over time (Gless 2015; Gless and Vervaele 2013). These processes must adapt to new developments in human rights enforcement, potentially at the expense of arguments favouring international comity or the need for enhanced transnational crime control that support a requesting nation's right to prosecute. A defendant-centred human rights emphasis can identify alternative pathways for the evolution of extradition law to meet these contemporary challenges, while restoring the key historical objective of protecting individuals from potential unfairness (Arnell 2013, 2018, 2019; Pyle 2001).

A defendant-centred approach to surrender might involve building specific requirements into extradition treaties that incorporate minimum international human rights standards. Reconciling diverse approaches to domestic due process requirements is potentially more complex. Here, extradition treaties could provide clearer guidance for domestic courts by allowing the state considering an extradition request to scrutinise certain elements of justice administration in the requesting state that are designed to promote fair trials, the rigorous scrutiny of and access to evidence before trial and the availability of adequate legal representation. Such considerations appear to have greater importance when human rights arguments are raised in cases where the alleged offending and the nationality of the extraditee are not immediately tied to either the state issuing or receiving the extradition request. Providing greater clarity on the relationship between human and due process rights in extradition treaties and domestic extradition laws can help guide national courts on specific criteria to promote greater international compliance with these important legal requirements. This emphasis can also help to erode the view that extradition is a contractual relationship between nation states and move towards a more even three-way relationship that incorporates greater consideration of international and domestic human rights issues that directly affect any extraditee.

Such measures are likely to enhance consistency when dealing with human rights arguments that currently have minimal weight in extradition decisions. They are also likely to contribute to a more coherent theory of global treaty compliance to help improve the development of transnational criminal law by offering clearer standards for national regulatory cooperation (Guzman 2002, 1826).

Additionally, this approach could alleviate pressures national courts face when deciding questions involving adherence to human rights or protective due process requirements in requesting states on a case-by-case basis (Gless 2013; Gless and Vervaele 2013). An integrated defendant-centred approach that recognises the centrality of international and domestic due process rights can assist with promoting enhanced uniformity and fairness in the absence of a generic or universally accepted rule regarding the status of human rights protection in the field of extradition law (Dugard and Van den Wyngaert 1998).

Clearly, such an emphasis alone is unlikely to rectify the problems identified in the cases described in this book. The objective in the remainder of this chapter is to propose two classes of reform that aim to offset the difficulties that emerge with reverse engineering theoretical and applied developments in extradition law from past decisions. The first focuses on changing existing approaches to extradition theory and practice. Our concern with these measures is based on the history of extensive reform to extradition law, which has had minimal impact in resolving the problems identified in this book. The second involves a more radical overhaul of the extradition process to enhance transnational criminal justice cooperation through open, transparent and neutral processes. This approach advocates for the development of new systems that revise the established theories and practices of extradition through what is termed the universalisation of criminal law and criminal jurisdiction.

Reforms to Current Extradition Process

The changes proposed in this section support research indicating government lawyers, senior prosecutors, defence counsel and judges from Australia, NZ, Canada, the US and Europe agree that human rights and individual protections are important considerations during the extradition process (Boister 2017a). Included are substantial reforms that enable shifting the forum for criminal trials to modify the entrenched principles of territorial sovereignty, introducing alternatives to established evidentiary requirements and enabling the oversight of the extraditee's ongoing welfare by states that have endorsed extradition requests.

Shifting the trial forum

Two key normative assumptions underpinning extradition are the requesting nation has a right to obtain the individual and the requested nation has an obligation to send the extraditee. If these presumptions are eliminated, it is possible more viable alternatives to the physical transfer of the extraditee could be developed. Shifting the trial forum, especially when most of the alleged offending occurred in the requested state, is one such option. This proposition would revise the normative assumption that an extraditee *must* be transferred to ensure that transnational justice is adequately administered, while mitigating various concerns held by extraditees regarding potential violations of international and due process rights that could compromise a fair trial or generate onerous conditions of pretrial and post-conviction imprisonment in a requesting state. Forum shifting would enable an extraditee to retain family and medical support systems that could be important to enhancing their welfare during protracted extradition and criminal proceedings or any post-conviction imprisonment.

Mann et al. (2018) highlight that shifting the trial forum to block an extraditee's surrender from the UK to the US would be useful in cases where the suspect has been diagnosed with autism spectrum disorder and allegedly committed the offences remotely through an online computer network. In circumstances where nations share concurrent jurisdiction for any related criminal offences, or where double criminality is clearly established, the trial could be held in the country where most of the harm originated. This would entail transferring evidence, rather than the individual, to the requested nation.

Forum shifting is reflected in the legal principle *aut dedere aut judicare* for both accused and convicted extraditees because it enables a state to deny extradition in exchange for prosecution or serving a sentence in a requested state (Plachta 1999, 139). However, 'forum shifting is consistently rejected as an avenue to protect transnational cybercrime suspects' and further research is needed to explore the practicality of introducing this option in other jurisdictions and extending its operation beyond transnational cyber offending that is attributed to the extraterritorial conduct of the extraditee (Mann et al. 2018, 116–17).

This approach could alleviate several issues raised by Assange concerning the potential mental health impacts of lengthy pretrial and post-conviction imprisonment in the US, which have been addressed through political assurances rather than clear legal rules aimed at protecting his rights. Forum shifting would also offset Savu's fears of persecution and the legal consequences of his refugee status, as well as limiting potential exposure to violations of the CAT stemming from the rule of non-inquiry in the Perez case. Forum shifting could also avert possible delays in determining extraditability, which would speed up the administration of justice in complex extradition and criminal cases. For example, the Assange and Dotcom cases have a degree of indeterminacy given both have spanned over a decade. Such delays slow down the process of reaching trial, which magnifies problems in recalling evidence and adds complexity to determining an appropriate sentence following surrender and conviction.

However, caution is needed when online testimony is required in extraterritorial trials. Research examining remote court proceedings necessitated by government-imposed lockdowns during the COVID-19 pandemic indicates virtual courts substantially alter the rituals of justice administration (see Rossner et al. 2021). Nevertheless, forum shifting can challenge the territorial limits of jurisdiction that are already stretched by the impact of globalisation in creating new and more frequent forms of transnational crime, as well as more complex extradition scenarios. While limiting disruption to the extraditee, forum shifting can add new forms of oversight to the administration of transnational criminal law in domestic legal systems.

Judicial and executive functions

As indicated earlier in this chapter, different national systems attribute varying weight to the judicial and executive decision-making in the field of extradition. Such variations undermine the development of a coherent approach to recognising human rights claims in extradition law, as judicial decisions form legal precedents on extradition law, whereas executive decisions are discretionary and non-binding. Ideally, judicial decision-making should be fostered to enhance the development of precedents that add both clarity and scope to how human rights standards are deemed applicable in extradition law.

Greater clarity in this area will help to promote consistency in understanding the relative roles of each branch of authority involved in the extradition process. This can begin to address the quasi-criminal nature of this procedure by helping to centre the judiciary's law-making function in developing strong precedents that deal with extradition and human rights. This can promote greater clarity in the rule of law related to extradition that potentially moves away from political comity as a key or sole factor in extradition decisions. While executive discretion should be maintained as it can offer meaningful protection of individual rights when judicial decisions are unwilling to do so (see Mann et al. 2018), greater consideration of rights-based arguments at the judicial stage generates a more publicly accountable approach to the development of extradition law.

Changes to evidentiary rules

An extradition hearing is not a criminal trial and is not designed to implement strict rules of evidence to prove an extraditee's guilt or innocence. This is a direct legacy of the quasi-criminal status of the judicial review function in extradition cases. To address this issue, Bassiouni (2003) has suggested US courts reviewing extradition requests should align the procedure with a conventional criminal process by incorporating the *Federal Rules of Criminal Procedure* (1944). Semmelman (1999) also recommended contradictory evidence should be admissible in extradition hearings if it enables a decision-maker to issue a summary ruling in the extraditee's favour under normal US civil standards of proof. This would 'help ensure the fairness of the extradition hearing, enhancing its due process function, without transforming the hearing into a trial on the merits' (Semmelman 1999, 1328).

The Diab case demonstrates how changes to evidentiary rules could help to protect an extraditee's due process rights. This case raised concerns about the reliability of evidence that might have been obtained through torture. Most of these issues were deemed inappropriate to examine in the Canadian extradition proceedings, while France determined the evidence was insufficient to formally instigate criminal charges following Diab's extradition in 2014, despite the subsequent *in absentia* conviction in 2023. Had different evidentiary rules applied under Canadian extradition law, the protracted legal proceedings and extensive time in custody Diab experienced could have been reduced.

The problem of admissibility of evidence is also clear in the Dotcom case. NZ courts ultimately ruled that evidence from the initial raid by NZ Police on Dotcom's property was unlawfully seized, duplicated and transferred to US authorities. However, an additional problem not argued in NZ proceedings relates to the admissibility of evidence obtained by US authorities from domestic or extraterritorial surveillance, or obtained with cooperation from the NZ Government Communications Security Bureau, that was listed in the record of the case accompanying the US extradition request. It was later discovered efforts to obtain much of this evidence also involved systematic violations of the privacy of many NZ citizens (Rogers 2023). This issue demonstrates extradition law is more concerned with the sufficiency of evidence to sustain the charges specified in the request, rather than the reliability or admissibility of evidence to support a possible conviction in the requesting state. The current emphasis can enable more problematic forms of transnational surveillance activity that are endorsed through networks of security agencies operating with minimal governmental accountability, while creating the risk that evidence derived from such activities might later be declared inadmissible during a criminal trial (Rogers 2023). Both the Diab and Dotcom cases suggest the reliability and admissibility of evidence supporting a request should be considered even if this adds time and complexity to extradition hearings.

Reviewing extraditee concerns

Several avenues for reform can also address extraditee concerns prior to surrender. Bassiouni (2003) recommended the rule of non-inquiry should be limited to enable courts to examine various human rights issues, such as the requesting state's practices of imprisonment and potential use of torture. Parry (2010, 1998) argued the rule of non-inquiry should be narrowed by allowing extradition courts to investigate 'fundamental claims' involving justice administration in requesting states, which could produce a humanitarian exception to surrender (Anderson 1983). If a court discovers any legal or procedural issues that compromise the protection of an extraditee's fundamental rights, this could provide grounds for limiting future governmental cooperation, while ensuring greater treaty compliance and reciprocity if individual rights protections are improved (de Felipe and Martín 2012; Guzman 2002, 2005; Magnuson 2012).

Closely aligned to problems with the rule of non-inquiry is a suggestion extradition courts should be allowed to actively review certain issues, such as the specialty principle, which confines prosecution to offences listed in the request, without the executive of the requested nation communicating with or seeking the permission of the requesting nation (Bassiouni 2003). Additionally, changes to allow a full appeal under US extradition law, rather than *habeas corpus* review which only focuses on whether the extraditee's imprisonment is lawful, have also been proposed (Bassiouni 2003).

The Perez case highlights the need for reform to the rule of non-inquiry. Here, concerns about a potential violation of the CAT, including the risk of Perez's torture and death, were considered beyond the scope of US courts to examine (see Baronia 2021). While critical scrutiny of the administration of justice in a foreign country and maintaining positive relationships between nations involves a delicate balance, limited rights-based inquiry could offset some of the more egregious consequences of surrender to ensure requesting nations meet clear human rights standards.

Greater post-extradition monitoring

A form of conditional extradition could enable a requested nation to monitor an extraditee's treatment following surrender to ensure relevant domestic and international human rights obligations are upheld, including the monitoring of assurances relating to the fair conduct of a criminal trial and the conditions of any pretrial or post-conviction incarceration (Dugard and Van den Wyngaert 1998; Rose 2002; Van Cleave 1999). Conditional surrender would also assist with the development of minimum human rights and due process standards by ensuring unacceptable conditions that breach diplomatic assurances from the requesting nation have a degree of external oversight (Johnston 2011, 30), while enhancing the prospect of compliance with international human rights and extradition treaties (Magnuson 2012; Van Cleave 1999, 29). However, as per the rule of non-inquiry, requesting nations are unlikely to agree with increased scrutiny of their domestic criminal justice processes, so this approach will only have meaningful impacts where states share mutually positive and trusting bi- and multilateral legal and political relationships (Dugard and Van den Wyngaert 1998).

Despite this limitation, many post-extradition concerns raised in the cases discussed in this book could be appropriately managed through conditional surrender and enhanced monitoring by requested states. For example, the UK could ensure Assange receives equivalent mental health treatment if surrendered to the US, while Canada and the US could monitor Savu and Perez, respectively, to limit the prospect of substantive rights violations. However, the process of monitoring the treatment of an extraditee following surrender does not necessarily mean maltreatment will be averted in all cases or could be remedied by the actions of a requested nation.

Sentence in the home nation

Shearer (1966) suggested the *locus delicti*, or the scene of the crime, is the proper place for a trial to occur. However, extradition could be limited to the trial only, with sentencing and imprisonment to be determined in the requested nation. This would ensure an extraditee would remain in close proximity to their family, society and culture. Alternatively, if the extraditee does not wish to return to their own nation, the punishment could be served in the prosecuting country as per normal extradition procedure.

Various international schemes allow foreign nationals imprisoned extraterritorially to serve a portion of their sentence in their home country, usually before they are deported from the nation where the conviction has been recorded (Kaufman 2017; Royce 2009). This process has also been incorporated into assurances to secure a person's extradition. For example, US justice officials have raised the possibility Assange could be given the option to return to Australia in exchange for pleas of guilty to some charges, although details of this offer remain unclear. In theory, this approach could address the concerns raised about US prison conditions by Assange and others accused of offshore cyber offences (see Mann et al. 2018) but would still limit the availability of important support networks during any pretrial detention or sentence served in the US. However, the McKinnon case illustrates such assurances can place onerous burdens on extraditees when linked to plea deals designed to entice their voluntary surrender (see Chapter 1). Stronger protocols or laws appear warranted in this area.

Harmonisation, Universalising Criminal Jurisdiction and a Transnational Criminal Court

The second area for extradition reform involves an extension of the concept of harmonisation in the form of universalising criminal jurisdiction and the related development of a Transnational Criminal Court (TCC). Such a radical revision of the extradition process is needed due to the clear limits of territorial theory in an era of global online communication and in light of the problematic impacts of extradition identified in this book. At the same time, any changes of this nature must gradually incorporate individual rights into agreed transnational laws, rather than remaining dependent on the will of individual nation states.

Harmonisation involves the convergence of national criminal laws, often in line with international demands in crime control treaties. This term commonly arises in the field of cybercrime, where multilateral treaties articulate base standards that signatory states should implement into their domestic criminal laws (Clough 2014). It is also common in EU criminal law, where centralised principles and human rights requirements aim to encourage nation states to reform their domestic laws to ensure consistency across this federation of nations to enhance the mutual recognition of judicial decisions (Mancano 2018; Sarmiento 2008).

Harmonisation moves away from a purely territorial approach to domestic criminal justice administration through the mutual incorporation of agreed offences and procedural standards into domestic law. Arguably, harmonisation has occurred with international crime, given genocide, crimes against humanity and war crimes have generated universal jurisdiction with agreed definitions incorporated into the criminal laws of most nations (Bassiouni 1974, 2014; Blakesley 1982, 1984, 2008; Harvard Research 1935). Bassiouni (2003, 405) favoured the harmonisation of extradition law by integrating a list of extraditable offences 'into a single comprehensive code of international cooperation'. Harmonisation can help to avoid unethical and unconstitutional practices stemming from national variations in the content and administration of the criminal law by eliminating the political vagaries of treaty-based extradition procedures and reciprocal executive agreements.

While harmonisation can enhance consistency in domestic extradition and criminal laws, national variations are still likely. This is because nations retain autonomy in the construction and administration of their laws. As the Dotcom case indicates, despite attempts at harmonising the laws of cyber offending, the double criminality test generates considerable technical complexity given the varied wording and content of different domestic criminal laws. These variations persist even if extradition law adopts an enumerative approach, where a specific class of extraditable offences is listed in a bi- or multilateral treaty.

Harmonisation can be taken further through a process of universalising criminal jurisdiction to specifically deal with the growing problem of transnational crime and the interrelated problems associated with extradition. Universalising jurisdiction draws from the idea of universal jurisdiction in international criminal law (Bassiouni 2014; Blakesley 2008). The aim of universalising jurisdiction is to develop a new method of articulating the content and administration of criminal law outside of existing national approaches, with the view of promoting genuine transnational coordination between nations, rather than relying on politically negotiated assurances, treaties and rules that require a requested nation to judge the merits of an accusation from a requesting state based on its own standards of legal and justice administration. The development of universal approaches to domestic criminal jurisdiction will help remove the fundamental problem emerging in extradition law where the connotations of the term 'fugitive' imply that judgment has already occurred. In reality, the extraditee is subject to an accusation raised in the extradition request that requires testing under the criminal law and related protection of the individual's rights. Rather than viewing such a convergence of criminal jurisdiction as ceding jurisdiction, which is common to current measures that promote cooperation between national justice systems, universalising jurisdiction should be viewed as a consolidation of national laws, procedures and jurisdictional rules that places harmonisation in a truly cooperative transnational sphere.

Universalising jurisdiction can promote the establishment of a TCC, as per Boister (2012). Much in the same way as the ECtHR influences domestic laws in the federation of EU nations, universalising jurisdiction can help to consolidate criminal laws and procedures through an agreed process of neutral judicial scrutiny. This will eliminate the need for extradition in some cases and 'present a solution for those jurisdictions seeking an alternative to extradition or prosecution' (Boister 2012, 296). A TCC would conduct trials as a neutral non-national forum, using agreed cross-fertilised procedures and criminal laws. A TCC could provide a more neutral system to limit political interference in cross-border cases and ensure an alternative mechanism exists when current methods of international cooperation break down. The TCC would 'not be a form of direct vertical enforcement against individuals but an international indirect horizontal system of enforcement', with each nation retaining the discretion to refer a case (Boister 2012, 313).

Extradition would be retained where a person is clearly a fugitive from the domestic jurisdiction of the requesting state, with a TCC focusing on extraterritorial cases and serious cases of systematic transnational offending. Rebane (1995) has advocated for a similarly structured court to safeguard individual rights at both international and transnational levels. This would help to promote neutrality in dealing with transnational crime problems, create greater uniformity, reduce political pressure, save time and reduce financial costs, while also functioning as a viable transnational enforcement mechanism.

Whilst universalising jurisdiction and the development of a TCC involve radical thinking, such approaches are necessary as criminal justice practitioners grapple with the challenges to sovereignty, territoriality and jurisdiction presented by enhanced transnationalism and globalisation. Shifting the way extradition is conceived will help transnational justice practitioners engage more readily with unified judicial and human rights values that should apply to any individual facing criminal charges. A coordinated approach could also prioritise the legal interests of the individual by providing greater protection for suspects involved in cross-border prosecutions (Gless 2015; Gless and Vervaele 2013).

Conclusion

The clear message of this book is to emphasise the complexity and hazards of extradition in twenty-first century society. Specifically, allegations of serious extraterritorial cyber offending, such as in the Assange and Dotcom cases, highlight the limits of a purely territorial approach to criminal jurisdiction, which is preserved by incremental modifications to the established process of extradition. While reforms to laws relating to evidentiary requirements and other due process standards can assist in improving extradition law, a workable TCC that universalises criminal jurisdiction offers a more radical alternative that can limit many of the individual rights dilemmas identified in this book and the extensive body of extradition research.

Conclusion

CHALLENGING THE NORMATIVE ASSUMPTIONS OF EXTRADITION

Introduction

This book does not aim to understate the severity of any offences or exaggerate the generalisability of the complex issues raised in the cases presented throughout. Rather, the goal is to highlight broader concerns about the protective aspects of extradition in contemporary global society that have been compromised by the skewed relationship between individual and state rights. The book argues the normative assumptions that determine how, why, when and against whom extradition operates must be re-examined in both their historical and contemporary forms to produce meaningful improvements to this branch of transnational criminal law. This chapter concludes by arguing a defendant-centred approach to extradition must adopt a revised series of normative assumptions that prioritise international human rights and domestic due process protections.

The Need for Reform

Extradition is an agreement between nation states reinforced through bi- or multilateral treaties. Judicial decisions examining individual rights do not sit readily within a contractual structure that prioritises political comity when examining the extension of national criminal jurisdiction beyond established territorial limits. While extradition treaties, and rules such as double criminality and specialty, offer qualified defendant-centred protection, extradition is ultimately an executive and political act. At times, executive decision-making can serve a protective function. As previous literature and the cases in this book demonstrate, this is not always reflected in the judicial process.

Chapters 2 and 3 indicate judicial outcomes examining the welfare of the extraditee or a nation's conduct overwhelmingly uphold the initial extradition request. This finding is partly explained by the tendency to frame the extraditee as a fugitive from the requesting state, rather than a person facing an accusation triggered by the request. The implications of the distinction are significant. A fugitive refers to an escapee or person subject to an *in absentia* conviction, who must be apprehended and surrendered to face the consequences of justice decisions that have already been made. By contrast, people facing accusations should be able to raise legally enforceable human rights and due process arguments in their defence. Research establishes the power to allege can be particularly onerous on domestic crime suspects (Pavlich and Unger 2017). This book's findings reinforce this trend, given the complexity and indeterminacy associated with legal challenges in complex extradition cases.

Courts seldom acknowledge individual human rights grounds as sufficient to successfully challenge an extradition request. A rare example is Assange's argument alleging his mental frailty could block extradition, which was ultimately overturned on appeal. Factors protected by international human rights or domestic due process requirements, such as poor or failing mental health and a high risk of suicide (Assange), fear of persecution and potential exposure to torture (Savu), violation of the CAT (Perez), the questionable legality of police actions (Dotcom), the use of unreliable evidence to support a request (Diab) and the inability to respond to communications between nations about the specialty principle (Snedden), were all rejected as grounds for surrender. The impacts of time delays, the extraditee's refugee status, a continued campaign for apprehension by the requesting nation and the application of the rule of non-inquiry, the double criminality test or political offence exception further illustrate the imbalance between individual rights and the priorities of international comity.

These outcomes show how extradition law prioritises the legal authority of the requesting nation to proceed with a criminal prosecution when an individual has allegedly infringed its domestic legislation (Blakesley 2008; Parry 2010), even if the alleged offending act was committed offshore such as in the Assange and Dotcom cases. This pattern reinforces the selective nature of international cooperation and political reciprocity in contemporary transnational criminal law through a cycle that prioritises the nation state as the key agent for promoting transnational justice cooperation (Abelson 2009; Cullen and Burgess 2015; Griffith and Harris 2005; Guzman 2002, 2005; Packer 1964; Van Cleave 1999; Williams 1992). Any significant consideration or enforcement of human rights and due process claims remains marginal despite consistent arguments highlighting their importance in promoting meaningful transnational justice cooperation (Arnell 2018; Dugard and Van den Wyngaert 1998; Magnuson 2012; Pyle 2001; Rose 2002). The elevation of bi- and multilateral policy interests over the legal rights of individuals establishes a form of 'coerced cooperation and dependency rather than interdependence' that undermines many protective elements embedded in the history of extradition law (Bifani 1993; Forst 2001, 166). This book's findings suggest that while territorial sovereignty remains the primary mechanism for administering cross-border justice in bi- and multilateral crime control and extradition treaties (Blakesley 2008; Magnuson 2012), human rights and due process arguments favouring the individual will continue to have limited weight in extradition decisions (Forstein 2015; Häkli 2013; Stamatel 2009; Warren and Palmer 2015; Wolitz 2013; Wong 1998).

Contract theory views treaties as agreements between states acting on behalf of their citizens or nationals (Moore 1891). These agreements are commonly informed by international and domestic political considerations with varied applied effects that depend on the nations involved, the nature of the alleged offending and the nationality of the extraditee (Magnuson 2012). Contract theory is also embedded in normative assumptions informing extradition law that validate the rule of non-inquiry (Bassiouni 2014; Pyle 2001), as well as three key aspects of extradition law that reflect its quasi-criminal nature:

1. The embedded role of political comity in executive decision-making and administrative law principles.
2. Legal adaptations to pretrial procedures that do not judge the guilt or innocence of the extraditee using admissible evidence, in deference to the integrity of the requesting nation's notions of criminal due process.
3. The role of international human rights requirements as compliance-based additions to existing laws and procedures, rather than requirements that are directly incorporated into the due process procedures of criminal justice systems.

Only a defendant-centred focus, or the more radical option of developing a neutral TCC, is likely to address these human rights concerns (Boister 2015; Dugard and Van den Wyngaert 1998; Gless 2015; Henning 1999). A defendant-centred approach views extradition as central to protecting the extraditee from potential human rights violations or an unfair trial in the requesting state (Gless 2015). The latter issue arose in the Assange and Dotcom cases, where the extraditees are either not nationals of the requesting or requested nations, or the allegedly harmful act occurred outside the jurisdictional territory of either country (Mann et al. 2018). These geographical nuances are directly tied to the centrality of territory to criminal jurisdiction, yet at the same time undermine rights-based arguments in contemporary extradition law.

Therefore, placing greater priority on the rights of the individual, or the development of a neutral TCC, requires shifting 'the criminological unit of analysis away from the jurisdictionally bounded state and on to more natural geographical regions' (Sheptycki 2011, 145).

The difficulty of reform

It is difficult to foresee the development of interdependent approaches to transnational justice that move beyond national and statist perspectives to achieve a balance between territorialism and universalism (Berman 2007; Forst 2001). While nations address transnational criminal cases through domestic laws and procedures, genuine cooperation will remain underdeveloped (Aas 2011b; Boister 2012; Bowling and Sheptycki 2015; Forst 2001; Gless 2013, 2015; Gless and Vervaele 2013; Stamatel 2009; Zumbansen 2010, 2012). Territorial sovereignty further inhibits this process because its entrenchment prevents the ability to think 'creatively about the way the law operates in an interconnected world' when addressing complex transnational crime control problems and the diverse perspectives of different actors during extradition (Berman 2005, 529).

Aas (2011a, 333) cautions against 'premature optimism' when contemplating the development of an 'integrated, harmonized and interoperable' transnational justice system, because of the 'obstacles to implementing a transnational law within the framework of state sovereignty' (Merry 2006, 977). Any future developments need to reconfigure established hierarchical and national crime control frameworks (Packer 1964; Roach 1999) while prioritising the rights of extraditees (Gless 2015). Barriers will persist as long as harmonisation or the development of a neutral transnational criminal law is viewed as ceding national legal sovereignty. This view mirrors the general level of scepticism towards a defendant-centred approach, given evident global concerns about the need for stronger transnational crime control measures that serve to validate state-centred aspects of extradition law, such as the rule of non-inquiry (Boister 2017a; Clough 2014; Cullen and Burgess 2015; Dugard and Van den Wyngaert 1998; Rose 2002).

Challenging the Normative Assumptions of Extradition

Specific reforms outlined in Chapter 4 aim to promote a defendant-centred approach to extradition. However, these measures must also challenge the underlying normative assumptions behind extradition law to ensure its 'jurisprudence [is] brought up to speed with extradition realities' (Bifani 1993, 693). Based on the six cases described in this book, the following revised normative assumptions are central to such a defendant-centred approach (Gless 2013).

- The extraditee is accused of a crime, rather than a crime having been committed.
- The extraditee has a right to legally challenge extradition by producing evidence of the trial approach and prison conditions in the requesting state.
- The extraditee is entitled to competent legal representation to enable a prompt, fair and rigorous challenge to an extradition request in line with agreed legal standards.
- The extradition process will recognise and comply with relevant international human rights requirements, such as the CAT, in line with any countervailing requirements in transnational crime control treaties.
- Where feasible, extradition decisions should be simplified to avoid unnecessary delays.
- Surrender is not the only or optimum outcome, and resources can be devoted to shifting the trial forum where appropriate.
- The requested state has an obligation to prosecute if the extraditee establishes their surrender is likely to create injustice, unfairness or a violation of recognised international human and due process protections in the requesting state.
- Extradition treaties should include clear justifications for the enumerative approach and a list of relevant parallel offences to assist with individual decisions.
- Greater efforts should be made to harmonise domestic criminal laws to meet international crime control demands in relevant treaties.

Placing such defendant-centred assumptions at the forefront of extradition law will help to enhance protection for suspects involved in cross-border prosecutions (Gless 2015; Gless and Vervaele 2013). It will also promote more balance between the rights of requesting states, the obligations of requested nations and the rights of the individual, which can limit predetermined decisions that favour the crime control interests of requesting nations (Packer 1964; Roach 1999; Sheptycki 2011).

Conclusion

Concerns over transnational crime control have outstripped the capacity of national justice systems to deal with these problems. Yet current legal responses to these issues through the laws of extradition understate the significance of enforceable human rights and due process protections. The cases examined in this book point to an imbalance within the existing structure of extradition law that clearly favours preserving international comity unless targeted or flagrant human rights breaches can be proved by extraditees when asserting their legal right to challenge a request. Only a radical revision to the normative assumptions behind extradition is likely to rectify this disparity through genuinely cooperative measures, such as the establishment of a neutral TCC, that are better equipped to embrace a more meaningful defendant-centred focus.

REFERENCES

Aas, Katja F. 2007. 'Analysing a World in Motion: Global Flows Meet "Criminology of the Other"'. *Theoretical Criminology* 11, no. 2: 283–303. https://doi.org/10.1177/1362480607075852.

———. 2011a. '"Crimmigrant" Bodies and Bona Fide Travelers: Surveillance, Citizenship and Global Governance'. *Theoretical Criminology* 15, no. 3: 331–46. https://doi.org/10.1177/1362480610396643.

———. 2011b. 'Visions of Global Control: Cosmopolitan Aspirations in a World of Friction'. In *What is Criminology?* edited by Mary Bosworth and Carolyn Hoyle, 406–19. Oxford: Oxford University Press. https://doi.org/10.1093/acprof:oso/9780199571826.003.0028.

———. 2012. '"The Earth is One but the World is Not": Criminological Theory and its Geopolitical Divisions'. *Theoretical Criminology* 16, no. 1: 5–20. https://doi.org/10.1177/1362480611433433.

Abbell, Michael. 2010. *Extradition To and From the United States 2010*. Netherlands: Martinus Nijhoff Publishers.

ABC News. 2019. 'Julian Assange Charged by US after Being Arrested by UK Police in Ecuadorian embassy'. 11 April. https://www.abc.net.au/news/2019-04-11/julian-assange-arrested-in-london/10995280.

Abelson, Adam B. 2009. 'The Prosecute/Extradite Dilemma: Concurrent Criminal Jurisdiction and Global Governance'. *UC Davis Journal of International Law & Policy* 16, no. 1: 1–38. https://papers.ssrn.com/sol3/papers.cfm?abstract_id=1477145.

Al Jazeera. 2023. 'French Court Convicts Canadian Professor for Synagogue Bombing'. 21 April. https://www.aljazeera.com/news/2023/4/21/french-court-convicts-canadian-professor-for-synagogue-bombing.

Allely, Clare S, Kennedy, Sally and Warren, Ian. 2022. 'Psychiatric and Legal Issues Surrounding the Extradition of WikiLeaks Founder Julian Assange: The Importance of Considering the Diagnosis of Autism Spectrum Disorder'. *Psychology, Public Policy, and Law* 28, no. 4: 630–43. https://doi.org/10.1037/law0000355.

Anderson, Leslie. 1983. 'Protecting the Rights of the Requested Person in Extradition Proceedings: An Argument for a Humanitarian Exception'. *Michigan Yearbook of International Legal Studies* 4, no 1: 153–72. https://repository.law.umich.edu/mjil/vol4/iss1/8.

Andreas, Peter and Nadelmann, Ethan A. 2006. *Policing the Globe: Criminalization and Crime Control in International Relations*. New York: Oxford University Press.

Angelson, Meredith 2009, 'Beyond the Myth of "Good Faith": Torture Evidence in International Extradition Hearings'. *New York University Journal of International Law and Politics* 41, no. 3: 603–53.

Antinucci, Mario. 2017. 'Life Sentence Penalty and Extradition under Article 3 of the ECHR: A Leading Case of the European Court of Human Rights'. *Iliria International Review* 7, no. 1: 119–27. https://doi.org/10.21113/iir.v7i1.288.

Arnell, Paul. 2013. 'The European Human Rights Influence upon UK Extradition: Myth Debunked'. *European Journal of Crime, Criminal Law and Criminal Justice* 21, no. 3–4: 317–37. https://doi.org/10.1163/15718174-21042032.

———. 2018. 'The Contrasting Evolution of the Right to a Fair Trial in UK Extradition Law'. *International Journal of Human Rights* 22, no. 7: 869–87. https://doi.org/10.1080/13642987.2018.1485655.

———. 2019. 'Extradition and Mental Health in UK Law'. *Criminal Law Forum* 30, 339–72. https://doi.org/10.1007/s10609-019-09369-7.

Attorney-General's Department. 2006. 'Attorney-General's Department Annual Report 2005–06'. *Australian Government.* https://webarchive.nla.gov.au/awa/20141216053941/https://www.ag.gov.au/Publications/AnnualReports/Annualreport200506/Pages/default.aspx.

———. 2011. 'Attorney-General's Department Annual Report 2010–11'. *Australian Government.* https://webarchive.nla.gov.au/awa/20191107004257/https://www.ag.gov.au/Publications/AnnualReports/Annualreport201011/Pages/default.aspx.

———. 2016. 'Attorney-General's Department Annual Report 2015–16'. *Australian Government.* https://webarchive.nla.gov.au/awa/20191107004644/https://www.ag.gov.au/Publications/AnnualReports/15-16/Pages/default.aspx.

———. 2022. 'Attorney-General's Department Annual Report 2021–22'. *Australian Government.* https://www.ag.gov.au/about-us/publications/attorney-generals-department-annual-report-2021-22.

Aughterson, Ned. 2005. 'The Extradition Process: An Unreviewable Executive Discretion'. *Australian Year Book of International Law* 24, 13–35. http://www5.austlii.edu.au/au/journals/AUYrBkIntLaw/2005/3.html.

Australian Associated Press. 2021. 'Julian Assange Could Serve Jail Term in Australia, Lawyer for the US Tells London Court'. 28 October. https://www.theguardian.com/media/2021/oct/28/julian-assange-could-serve-jail-term-in-australia-lawyer-for-the-us-tells-london-court.

Baronia, Nitisha. 2021. 'Reviewing Extraditions to Torture'. *Stanford Law Review* 73, no. 5: 1221–87. https://www.stanfordlawreview.org/print/article/reviewing-extraditions-to-torture/.

Bassiouni, Mahmoud C. 1974. 'Theories of Jurisdiction and Their Application in Extradition Law and Practice'. *California Western International Law Journal* 5, no. 1: 1–61. https://scholarlycommons.law.cwsl.edu/cgi/viewcontent.cgi?article=1927&context=cwilj.

———. 1984. 'A Conceptual Framework for Extradition and Jurisdiction over Extraterritorial Crimes'. *Utah Law Review* 1984, no. 4: 685–761. https://scholars.law.unlv.edu/facpub/319/.

———. 2003. 'Reforming International Extradition: Lessons of the Past for a Radical New Approach'. *Loyola of Los Angeles International and Comparative Law Review* 25, no. 3: 389–408. https://www.legal-tools.org/doc/62caa6/pdf/.

———. 2008. 'Law and Practice of the United States'. In *International Criminal Law: Volume II: Multilateral and Bilateral Enforcement Mechanisms* (3rd edn), edited by Mahmoud C. Bassiouni, 269–341. Netherlands: Martinus Nijhoff Publishers.

———. 2014. *International Extradition: United States Law and Practice* (6th edn). Oxford: Oxford University Press.

Berman, Paul S. 2005. 'From International Law to Law and Globalization'. *Columbia Journal of Transnational Law* 43, no. 2: 485–556. https://scholarship.law.gwu.edu/cgi/viewcontent.cgi?article=1078&context=faculty_publications.

———. 2007. 'Global Legal Pluralism'. *Southern California Law Review* 80, no. 6: 1155–238. https://southerncalifornialawreview.com/wp-content/uploads/2018/01/80_1155.pdf.

———. 2012. *Global Legal Pluralism: A Jurisprudence of Law Beyond Borders*. New York: Cambridge University Press.

Bifani, Darin A. 1993. 'The Tension between Policy Objectives and Individual Rights: Rethinking Extradition and Extraterritorial Abduction Jurisprudence'. *Buffalo Law Review* 41, no. 2: 627–702. https://digitalcommons.law.buffalo.edu/buffalolawreview/vol41/iss2/5/.

Blakesley, Christopher L. 1980. 'Extradition between France and the United States: An Exercise in Comparative and International Law'. *Vanderbilt Journal of Transnational Law* 13, no. 4: 653–716. https://scholarship.law.vanderbilt.edu/vjtl/vol13/iss3/1/.

———. 1981. 'The Practice of Extradition from Antiquity to Modern France and the United States: A Brief History'. *Boston College International and Comparative Law Review* 4, no. 1: 39–60. https://scholars.law.unlv.edu/facpub/317/.

———. 1982. 'United States Jurisdiction over Extraterritorial Crime'. *The Journal of Criminal Law and Criminology* 73, no. 3: 1109–63. https://doi.org/10.2307/1143188.

———. 1984. 'A Conceptual Framework for Extradition and Jurisdiction over Extraterritorial Crimes'. *Utah Law Review* 1984, no. 4: 685–761. https://scholars.law.unlv.edu/facpub/319/.

———. 2000. 'Autumn of the Patriarch: The Pinochet Extradition Debacle and Beyond: Human Rights Clauses Compared to Traditional Derivative Protections such as Double Criminality'. *Journal of Criminal Law and Criminology* 91, no. 1: 1–98. https://doi.org/10.2307/1144146.

———. 2008. 'Extraterritorial Jurisdiction'. In *International Criminal Law: Volume II: Multilateral and Bilateral Enforcement Mechanisms* (3rd edn), edited by Mahmoud C. Bassiouni, 85–152. Netherlands: Martinus Nijhoff Publishers.

Blakesley, Christopher L. and Lagodny, Otto. 1991. 'Finding Harmony amidst Disagreement over Extradition, Jurisdiction, the Role of Human Rights, and Issues of Extraterritoriality under International Criminal Law'. *Vanderbilt Journal of Transnational Law* 24, no. 1: 1–74. https://scholarship.law.vanderbilt.edu/cgi/viewcontent.cgi?article=1993&context=vjtl.

Bloom, Matthew. 2008. 'A Comparative Analysis of the United States's Response to Extradition Requests from China'. *Yale Journal of International Law* 33, no. 1: 177–214. https://openyls.law.yale.edu/handle/20.500.13051/6563.

Boister, Neil. 2003. '"Transnational Criminal Law?"' *European Journal of International Law* 14, no. 5: 953–76. https://doi.org/10.1093/ejil/14.5.953.

———. 2012. 'International Tribunals for Transnational Crimes: Towards a Transnational Criminal Court?' *Criminal Law Forum* 23, no. 4: 295–318. https://doi.org/10.1007/s10609-012-9182-4.

———. 2015. 'Further Reflections on the Concept of Transnational Criminal Law'. *Transnational Legal Theory* 6, no. 1: 9–30. https://doi.org/10.1080/20414005.2015.1042232.

———. 2017a. 'Global Simplification of Extradition: Interviews with Selected Extradition Experts in New Zealand, Canada, the US and EU'. *Criminal Law Forum* 29, no. 3: 327–75. https://doi.org/10.1007/s10609-017-9342-7.

———. 2017b. 'Law Enforcement Cooperation between New Zealand and the United States: Serving the Internet "Pirate" Kim Dotcom up on a Silver Platter?' In *Trust in International Police and Justice Cooperation*, edited by Saskia Hufnagel and Carole McCartney, 193–220. UK: Hart Publishing.

———. 2023. 'A History of Double Criminality in Extradition'. *Journal of the History of International Law* 25, no. 2: 218–57. https://doi.org/10.1163/15718050-bja10089.

Botting, Gary. 2005. *Extradition between Canada and the United States*. New York: Transnational Publishers.

———. 2015. *Canadian Extradition Law Practice* (5th edn). Ontario: LexisNexis Canada.

Bowling, Ben. 2011. 'Transnational Criminology and the Globalization of Harm Production'. In *What is Criminology?* edited by Mary Bosworth and Carolyn Hoyle, 361–79. Oxford: Oxford University Press. https://doi.org/10.1093/acprof:oso/9780199571826.003.0025.

Bowling, Ben and Sheptycki, James. 2015. 'Global Policing and Transnational Rule with Law'. *Transnational Legal Theory* 6, no. 1: 141–73. https://doi.org/10.1080/20414005.2015.1042235.

Brewster, Rachel. 2004. 'The Domestic Origins of International Agreements'. *Virginia Journal of International Law* 44, no. 2: 501–44. https://scholarship.law.duke.edu/cgi/viewcontent.cgi?article=5319&context=faculty_scholarship.

Butterly, Nick. 2017. 'Accused Perth War Criminal Charles Zentai was "a Loving Man" Claim Family'. *The West Australian*, 21 December. https://thewest.com.au/news/perth/accused-perth-war-criminal-charles-zentai-was-a-loving-man-claim-family-ng-b88695878z.

Buxbaum, Hannah L. 2009. 'Territory, Territoriality, and the Resolution of Jurisdictional Conflict'. *American Journal of Comparative Law* 57, no. 3: 631–75. https://doi.org/10.5131/ajcl.2008.0018.

Carrington, Kerry, Hogg, Russell and Sozzo, Máximo. 2016. 'Southern Criminology'. *British Journal of Criminology* 56, no. 1: 1–20, https://doi.org/10.1093/bjc/azv083.

Chan, Janet. 2000. 'Globalisation, Reflexivity and the Practice of Criminology'. *Australian and New Zealand Journal of Criminology* 33, no. 2: 118–35. https://doi.org/10.1177/000486580003300202.

Clough, Jonathan. 2014. 'A World of Difference: The Budapest *Convention on Cybercrime* and the Challenges of Harmonisation'. *Monash University Law Review* 40, no. 3: 698–736. https://www.monash.edu/__data/assets/pdf_file/0019/232525/clough.pdf.

CNW. 2023. 'Lawsuit by Hassan Diab over 2014 Extradition to France Discontinued with Prejudice'. 25 August. https://www.newswire.ca/news-releases/lawsuit-by-hassan-diab-over-2014-extradition-to-france-discontinued-with-prejudice-842896263.html.

Cochrane, David and Laventure, Lisa. 2018. 'France Told Canada Key Evidence Did Not Exist in Hassan Diab Terrorism Case'. *CBC News*, 21 June. https://www.cbc.ca/news/politics/hassan-diab-france-evidence-1.4714307.

Colquhoun, Charles. 2000. 'Human Rights and Extradition Law in Australia'. *Australian Journal of Human Rights* 6, no. 2: 1–19. http://www.austlii.edu.au/au/journals/AUJlHRights/2000/22.html.

Connell, Raewyn and Dados, Nour. 2014. 'Where in the World does Neoliberalism come from?' *Theory and Society* 43, no. 2: 117–38. https://doi.org/10.1007/s11186-014-9212-9.

Corbett, William H. 2002. 'The 125 Year History of Canada's Extradition Statutes and Treaties'. *Commonwealth Law Bulletin* 28, no. 1: 497–546. https://doi.org/10.1080/03050718.2002.9986616.

Cotterrell, Roger. 2012. 'What is Transnational Law?' *Law & Social Inquiry* 37, no. 2: 500–24. https://doi.org/10.1111/j.1747-4469.2012.01306.x.

Cullen, Holly and Burgess, Bethia. 2015. 'Extradition from A to Z: Assange, Zentai and the Challenge of Interpreting International Obligations'. *University of Western Australia Law Review* 39, no. 2: 208–38. https://www.law.uwa.edu.au/__data/assets/pdf_file/0005/2795576/Extradition-from-A-to-Z.pdf.

Daigle, Thomas and Cochrane, David. 2018. 'Renewed Calls for Public Inquiry as France Pushes Appeal Decision in Hassan Diab Case to Next Year'. *CBC News*, 27 October. https://www.cbc.ca/news/politics/diab-france-terrorism-appeal-1.4878064.

Daskal, Jennifer. 2015. 'The Un-Territoriality of Data'. *Yale Law Journal* 125, no. 2: 326–98. https://www.yalelawjournal.org/article/the-un-territoriality-of-data.

———. 2017. 'Law Enforcement Access to Data across Borders: The Evolving Security and Human Rights Issues'. *Journal of National Security Law and Policy* 8, 473–501. https://jnslp.com/wp-content/uploads/2017/10/Law-Enforcement-Access-to-Data-Across-Borders_2.pdf.

de Felipe, Miguel B and Martín, Adán N. 2012. 'Post 9/11 Trends in International Judicial Cooperation: Human Rights as a Constraint on Extradition in Death Penalty Cases'. *Journal of International Criminal Justice* 10, no. 3: 581–604. https://doi.org/10.1093/jicj/mqs041.

Dorsett, Shaunnagh and McVeigh, Shaun. 2012. *Jurisdiction*. New York: Routledge.

Dugard, John and Van den Wyngaert, Christine. 1998. 'Reconciling Extradition with Human Rights'. *American Journal of International Law* 92, no. 2: 187–212. https://doi.org/10.2307/2998029.

Edmonds-Poli, Emily and Shirk, David. 2018. 'Extradition as a Tool for International Cooperation: Lessons from the U.S.-Mexico Relationship'. *Maryland Journal of International Law* 33, no. 1: 215–43. https://digitalcommons.law.umaryland.edu/mjil/vol33/iss1/10.

Efrat, Asif and Newman, Abraham. 2020. 'Defending Core Values: Human Rights and the Extradition of Fugitives'. *Journal of Peace Research* 57, no. 4: 581–96. https://doi.org/10.1177/0022343319898231.

Epps, Valerie. 2003. 'The Development of the Conceptual Framework Supporting International Extradition'. *Loyola of Los Angeles International and Comparative Law Review* 25, no. 3: 369–87. https://digitalcommons.lmu.edu/cgi/viewcontent.cgi?article=1545&context=ilr.

European Court of Human Rights (ECtHR) Press Unit. 2023. 'Factsheet – Extradition and Life Imprisonment'. *European Court of Human Rights*. https://www.echr.coe.int/documents/d/echr/fs_extradition_life_sentence_eng#:~:text=Regarding%20the%20risk%20of%20life,that%20there%20would%20be%20a.

Forst, Rainer. 2001. 'Towards a Critical Theory of Transnational Justice'. *Metaphilosophy* 32, no. 1–2: 160–79. https://doi.org/10.1111/1467-9973.00180.

Forstein, Carolyn. 2015. 'Challenging Extradition: The Doctrine of Specialty in Customary International Law'. *Columbia Journal of Transnational Law* 53, no. 2: 363–95. https://papers.ssrn.com/sol3/papers.cfm?abstract_id=2410467.

Foster, Steve H. 2015. 'Whole Life Sentences and Article 3 of the European Convention on Human Rights: Times for Certainty and a Common Approach?' *Liverpool Law Review* 36, 147–69. https://doi.org/10.1007/s10991-015-9166-7.

Friedrichs, David O. 2007. 'Transnational Crime and Global Criminology: Definitional, Typological, and Contextual Conundrums'. *Social Justice* 34, no. 2: 4–15. https://www.jstor.org/stable/29768431.

Garcia-Mora, Manuel R. 1962. 'War Crimes and the Principle of Non-Extradition of Political Offenders'. *Wayne Law Review* 9, no. 2: 269–307. https://heinonline.org/HOL/LandingPage?handle=hein.journals/waynlr9&div=37&id=&page=.

Garland, David. 1996. 'The Limits of the Sovereign State: Strategies of Crime Control in Contemporary Society'. *British Journal of Criminology* 36, no. 4: 445–71. https://doi.org/10.1093/oxfordjournals.bjc.a014105.

Gless, Sabine. 2013. 'Transnational Cooperation in Criminal Matters and the Guarantee of a Fair Trial: Approaches to a General Principle'. *Utrecht Law Review* 9, no. 4: 90–108. https://doi.org/10.18352/ulr.244.

———. 2015. 'Bird's-Eye View and Worm's-Eye View: Towards a Defendant-Based Approach in Transnational Criminal Law'. *Transnational Legal Theory* 6, no. 1: 117–40. https://doi.org/10.1080/20414005.2015.1042233.

Gless, Sabine and Vervaele, John A. E. 2013. 'Law Should Govern: Aspiring General Principles for Transnational Criminal Justice'. *Utrecht Law Review* 9, no. 4: 1–10. https://doi.org/10.18352/ulr.239.

Goldsmith, Jack L. and Posner, Eric A. 1999. 'A Theory of Customary International Law'. *University of Chicago Law Review* 66, no. 4: 1113–77. https://chicagounbound.uchicago.edu/cgi/viewcontent.cgi?article=2767&context=journal_articles.

———. 2003. 'International Agreements: A Rational Choice Approach'. *Virginia Journal of International Law* 44, no. 1: 113–44. https://chicagounbound.uchicago.edu/cgi/viewcontent.cgi?article=2793&context=journal_articles.

Green, Leslie C. 1962. 'Political Offences, War Crimes and Extradition'. *International & Comparative Law Quarterly* 11, no. 2: 329–54. https://doi.org/10.1093/iclqaj/11.2.329.

Gregg, Robert. 2002. 'The European Tendency toward Non-Extradition to the United States in Capital Cases: Trends, Assurances, and Breaches of Duty'. *University of Miami International and Comparative Law Review* 10, no. 2: 113–28. https://repository.law.miami.edu/umiclr/vol10/iss1/9.

Griffith, Gavan and Harris, Claire. 2005. 'Recent Developments in the Law of Extradition'. *Melbourne Journal of International Law* 6, no. 1: 33–54. https://law.unimelb.edu.au/__data/assets/pdf_file/0007/1681144/Griffith-and-Harris.pdf.

Guzman, Andrew T. 2002. 'A Compliance-Based Theory of International Law'. *California Law Review* 90, no. 6: 1823–87. https://doi.org/10.15779/Z388728.

———. 2005. 'The Design of International Agreements'. *European Journal of International Law* 16, no. 4: 579–612. https://doi.org/doi:10.1093/ejil/chi134.

Hagan, John and Ivković, Sanja K. 2006. 'War Crimes, Democracy, and the Rule of Law in Belgrade, the Former Yugoslavia and Beyond'. *Annals of the American Academy of Political and Social Science* 605, no. 1: 130–51. https://doi.org/10.1177/0002716206287088.

Haig, Terry. 2020. 'Hassan Diab Files Multi-Million Suit against Federal Government'. *Radio Canada International*, 14 January. https://www.rcinet.ca/en/2020/01/14/hassan-diab-files-multi-million-suit-against-federal-government/.

Häkli, Jouni. 2013. 'State Space: Outlining a Field Theoretical Approach'. *Geopolitics* 18, no. 2: 343–55. https://doi.org/10.1080/14650045.2012.723285.

Harrington, Joanna. 2005. 'The Role for Human Rights Obligations in Canadian Extradition Law'. *Canadian Yearbook of International Law* 43, 45–100. https://doi.org/10.1017/S0069005800008742.

Harvard Research. 1935. 'Draft Convention on Jurisdiction with Respect to Crime'. *The American Journal of International Law* 29, 439–42. https://doi.org/10.2307/2213634.

Harvie, Robert and Foster, Hamar. 2005. 'Shocks and Balances: *United States v. Burns*, Fine-Tuning Canadian Extradition Law and the Future of the Death Penalty'. *Gonzaga Law Review* 40, no.2: 293–327. https://blogs.gonzaga.edu/gulawreview/files/2011/02/HarvieFoster.pdf.

Henning, Matthew W. 1999. 'Extradition Controversies: How Enthusiastic Prosecutions Can Lead to International Incidents'. *Boston College International and Comparative Law Review* 22, no. 2: 347–81. https://lira.bc.edu/work/ns/f12eea44-b634-4b6c-9f35-363025b0336a.

Higgins, Rosalyn. 2009. *Themes and Theories: Selected Essays, Speeches, and Writing in International Law*. Oxford: Oxford University Press.

Iraola, Roberto. 2009. 'Foreign Extradition and In Absentia Convictions'. *Seton Hall Law Review* 39, no. 3: 843–59. https://scholarship.shu.edu/cgi/viewcontent.cgi?article=1021&context=shlr.

Ireland-Piper, Danielle. 2012. 'Extraterritorial Criminal Jurisdiction: Does the Long Arm of the Law Undermine the Rule of Law?' *Melbourne Journal of International Law* 13, no. 1: 122–57. https://law.unimelb.edu.au/__data/assets/pdf_file/0007/1687246/Ireland-Piper.pdf.

Johnston, Jeffrey G. 2011. 'The Risk of Torture as a Basis for Refusing Extradition and the Use of Diplomatic Assurances to Protect against Torture after 9/11'. *International Criminal Law Review* 11, no. 1: 1–48. https://doi.org/10.1163/157181211X543911.

Karhula, Päivikki. 2011. 'What is the Effect of WikiLeaks for Freedom of Information?' *International Federation of Library Associations*. https://www.ifla.org/publications/what-is-the-effect-of-wikileaks-for-freedom-of-information/.

Karstedt, Susanne. 2001. 'Comparing Cultures, Comparing Crime: Challenges, Prospects, and Problems for a Global Criminology'. *Crime, Law and Social Change* 36, no. 3: 285–308. https://doi.org/10.1023/A:1012223323445.

Kaufman, Emma. 2017. 'Extraterritorial Punishment'. *New Criminal Law Review* 20, no. 1: 66–95. https://doi.org/10.1525/nclr.2017.20.1.66.

Kennedy, Sally and Warren, Ian. 2020. 'The Legal Geographies of Extradition and Sovereign Power'. *Internet Policy Review* 9, no. 3: 1–18. https://doi.org/10.14763/2020.3.1496.

————. 2022. 'Extraterritorial Offending, Extradition and the Case against Hew Griffiths'. *International Journal of Comparative and Applied Criminal Justice* 47, no. 3: 299–315. https://doi.org/10.1080/01924036.2021.2023026.

King, Evan. 2015. 'The Effect of the United Nations Convention against Torture on the Scope of Habeas Review in the Context of International Extradition'. *Fordham International Law Journal* 38, no. 3: 779–824. https://ir.lawnet.fordham.edu/ilj/vol38/iss3/4/.

Knott, Matthew. 2023. '"He Could Die in Jail": Labor Luminaries Urge Albanese to Step Up Assange Efforts'. *The Sydney Morning Herald*, 14 August. https://www.smh.com.au/politics/federal/he-could-die-in-jail-labor-luminaries-urge-albanese-to-step-up-assange-efforts-20230814-p5dwbj.html.

Koh, Harold H 1996. 'The 1994 Roscoe Pound Lecture: Transnational Legal Process'. *Nebraska Law Review* 75, no. 1: 181–208. https://digitalcommons.unl.edu/cgi/viewcontent.cgi?article=1538&context=nlr.

Labardini, Rodrigo. 2005. 'Life Imprisonment and Extradition: Historical Development, International Content, and the Current Situation in Mexico and the United States'. *Southwestern Journal of Law and Trade in the Americas* 11, no. 1: 1–108. https://heinonline.org/HOL/LandingPage?handle=hein.journals/sjlta11&div=6&id=&page=.

Leeson, Jami. 1996. 'Refusal to Extradite: An Examination of Canada's Indictment of the American Legal System'. *Georgia Journal of International and Comparative Law* 25, no. 3: 641–58. https://digitalcommons.law.uga.edu/gjicl/vol25/iss3/8/.

Loader, Ian and Percy, Sarah. 2012. 'Bringing the "Outside" In and the "Inside" Out: Crossing the Criminology/IR Divide'. *Global Crime* 13, no. 4: 213–8. https://doi.org/10.1080/17440572.2012.715402.

MacNaughton, Gillian and Duger, Angela. 2020. 'Translating International Law into Domestic Law, Policy, and Practice'. In *Foundations of Global Health & Human Rights*, edited by Lawrence O. Gostin and Benjamin M. Meier, 113–32. Oxford: Oxford University Press. https://doi.org/10.1093/oso/9780197528297.003.0006.

Magnay, Jacquline, Profaca, Ivica and Pantovic, Milivoje. 2020. 'War Criminal Captain Dragan Vasiljkovic Released from Prison, Eyes Political Career'. *The Australian*, 29 March. https://www.theaustralian.com.au/world/war-criminal-captain-draganvasiljkovic-released-from-prison-eyes-political-career/newsstory/382893725ddffe0e5caaaad633ae14b1.

Magnuson, William. 2012. 'The Domestic Politics of International Extradition'. *Virginia Journal of International Law* 52, no. 4: 839–901. https://scholarship.law.tamu.edu/facscholar/757.

Mancano, Leandron. 2018. 'Judicial Harmonisation through Autonomous Concepts of European Union Law: The Example of the European Arrest Warrant Framework Decision'. *European Law Review* 43, no. 1: 69–88. https://papers.ssrn.com/sol3/papers.cfm?abstract_id=3355699.

Mann, Monique and Warren, Ian. 2018. 'The Digital and Legal Divide: Silk Road, Transnational Online Policing and Southern Criminology'. In *The Palgrave Handbook of Criminology and the Global South*, edited by in Kerry Carrington, Russell Hogg, John Scott and Máximo Sozzo, 245–60. London: Palgrave Macmillan. https://doi.org/10.1007/978-3-319-65021-0.

Mann, Monique, Warren, Ian and Kennedy, Sally. 2018. 'The Legal Geographies of Transnational Cyber-Prosecutions: Extradition, Human Rights and Forum Shifting'. *Global Crime* 19, no. 2: 107–24. https://doi.org/10.1080/17440572.2018.1448272.

Marmo, Marinella and Chazal, Nerida. 2016. *Transnational Crime and Justice*. Los Angeles: SAGE.

May, Theresa. 2012. 'Theresa May Statement on Gary McKinnon Extradition'. *Home Office*, 16 October. https://www.gov.uk/government/news/theresa-may-statement-on-gary-mckinnon-extradition.

Melzer, Nils. 2022. *The Trial of Julian Assange: A Story of Persecution*. London: Verso.

Melzer, Nils and Aoláin, Fionnuala N. 2020. 'Mandates of the Special Rapporteur on Torture and Other Cruel, Inhuman or Degrading Treatment or Punishment and the Special Rapporteur on the Promotion and Protection of Human Rights and Fundamental Freedoms while Countering Terrorism'. *The United Nations Office at Geneva*, 16 December. https://spcommreports.ohchr.org/TMResultsBase/DownLoadPublicCommunicationFile?gId=25771.

Merry, Sally E. 1988. 'Legal Pluralism'. *Law & Society Review* 22, no. 5: 869–96. https://doi.org/10.2307/3053638.

———. 2006. 'New Legal Realism and the Ethnography of Transnational Law'. *Law and Social Inquiry* 31, no. 4: 975–98. https://doi.org/10.1111/j.1747-4469.2006.00042.x.

Miller, Bradley. 2009. '"A Carnival of Crime on Our Border": International Law, Imperial Power, and Extradition in Canada, 1865–1883'. *Canadian Historical Review* 90, no. 4: 639–69. https://doi.org/10.3138/chr.90.4.639.

———. 2016, *Borderline Crime: Fugitive Criminals and the Challenge of the Border, 1819–1914*. Toronto: University of Toronto Press.

Moore, John B. 1891. *A Treatise of Extradition and Interstate Rendition*. Boston: The Boston Book Company.

Murchison, Matthew. 2007. 'Extradition's Paradox: Duty, Discretion, and Rights in the World of Non-Inquiry'. *Stanford Journal of International Law* 43, no. 2: 295–318. https://papers.ssrn.com/sol3/papers.cfm?abstract_id=1554975.

Nadelmann, Ethan A. 1990. 'Global Prohibition Regimes: The Evolution of Norms in International Society'. *International Organization* 44, no. 4: 479–526. https://doi.org/10.1017/S0020818300035384.

Natarajan, Mangai, ed. 2019. *International and Transnational Crime and Justice* (2nd edn). Cambridge: Cambridge University Press.

Nelken, David. 2011. 'Afterword: Studying Criminal Justice in Globalising Times'. In *Comparative Criminal Justice and Globalization*, edited by David Nelken, 183–210. UK: Routledge.

Neumann, Robert G. 1951. 'Neutral States and the Extradition of War Criminals'. *American Journal of International Law* 45, no. 3: 495–508. https://doi.org/10.2307/2194546.

Office of the High Commissioner for Human Rights. 1997. 'CAT General Comment No. 1: Implementation of Article 3 of the Convention in the Context of Article 22 (Refoulment and Communications)'. *Committee against Torture*, 21 November. https://www.refworld.org/pdfid/453882365.pdf.

Orchard, Phil. 2017. 'The Dawn of International Refugee Protection: States, Tacit Cooperation and Non-Extradition'. *Journal of Refugee Studies* 30, no. 2: 282–300. https://doi.org/10.1093/jrs/few014.

Packer, Herbert L. 1964. 'Two Models of the Criminal Process'. *University of Pennsylvania Law Review* 113, no. 1: 1–68. https://scholarship.law.upenn.edu/cgi/viewcontent.cgi?article=6428&context=penn_law_review.

Palmer, Darren and Warren, Ian. 2013. 'Global Policing and the Case of Kim Dotcom'. *International Journal for Crime, Justice and Social Democracy* 2, no. 3: 105–19. https://doi.org/10.5204/ijcjsd.v2i3.105.

Palmer, Nicola. 2015. *Courts in Conflict: Interpreting the Layers of Justice in Post-Genocide Rwanda*. New York: Oxford University Press.

Parry, John T. 2010. 'International Extradition, the Rule of Non-Inquiry, and the Problem of Sovereignty'. *Boston University Law Review* 90, no. 5: 1973–2029. https://papers.ssrn.com/sol3/papers.cfm?abstract_id=1508019.

Pavlich, George and Unger, Matthew P., eds. 2017. *Accusation: Creating Criminals*. Vancouver: University of British Columbia Press.

Petersen, Antje C. 1992. 'Extradition and the Political Offence Exception in the Suppression of Terrorism'. *Indiana Law Journal* 67, no. 3: 767–97. https://www.repository.law.indiana.edu/ilj/vol67/iss3/6.

Pilkington, Ed. 2024. 'Julian Assange Released From Prison, Wikileaks Says, After Striking Deal With US Justice Department'. *The Guardian*, 25 June. https://www.theguardian.com/media/article/2024/jun/25/julian-assange-plea-deal-with-us-free-to-return-australia.

Piragoff, Donald and Kran, Marcia. 1992. 'The Impact of Human Rights Principles on Extradition from Canada and the United States: The Role of National Courts'. *Criminal Law Forum* 3, no. 2: 225–70. https://doi.org/10.1007/BF01096200.

Plachta, Michael. 1999. '(Non-)Extradition of Nationals: A Neverending Story?' *Emory International Law Review* 13, 77–159. https://heinonline.org/HOL/LandingPage?handle=hein.journals/emintl13&div=7&id=&page=.

Pyle, Christopher H. 2001. *Extradition, Politics, and Human Rights*. Philadelphia: Temple University Press.

Quigley, John. 1990. 'The Rule of Non-Inquiry and the Impact of Human Rights on Extradition Law'. *North Carolina Journal of International Law and Commercial Regulation* 15, no. 3: 401–44. https://scholarship.law.unc.edu/cgi/viewcontent.cgi?article=1422&context=ncilj.

———. 1996. 'The Rule of Non-Inquiry and Human Rights Treaties'. *Catholic University Law Review* 45, no. 4: 1213–48. https://scholarship.law.edu/lawreview/vol45/iss4/3.

Quinn, Ben. 2019. 'Sweden Drops Julian Assange Rape Investigation'. *The Guardian*, 20 November. https://www.theguardian.com/media/2019/nov/19/sweden-drops-julian-assange-investigation.

Raustiala, Kal. 2009. *Does the Constitution Follow the Flag?:The Evolution of Territoriality in American Law*. Oxford: Oxford University Press. https://doi.org/10.1093/oso/9780195304596.001.0001.

Rebane, Kai I. 1995. 'Extradition and Individual Rights: The Need for an International Criminal Court to Safeguard Individual Rights'. *Fordham International Law Journal* 19, no. 4: 1636–85. https://ir.lawnet.fordham.edu/cgi/viewcontent.cgi?article=1507&context=ilj.

Rebaza, Claudia and Said-Moorhouse, Lauren. 2023. 'Julian Assange Loses Latest Attempt to Appeal against Extradition to the US'. *CNN*, 9 June. https://edition.cnn.com/2023/06/09/uk/julian-assange-extradition-appeal-intl-gbr/index.html.

Roach, Kent. 1999. 'Four Models of the Criminal Process'. *The Journal of Criminal Law and Criminology* 89, no. 2: 671–716. https://scholarlycommons.law.northwestern.edu/cgi/viewcontent.cgi?article=7000&context=jclc.

Roberg, Jeffery L. 2007. 'The Importance of International Treaties: Is Ratification Necessary?' *World Affairs* 169, no. 4: 181–86. https://www.jstor.org/stable/20672774.

Rogers, Damien. 2023. 'The Anatomy of Political Impunity in New Zealand'. In *Intelligence Oversight in Times of Transnational Impunity: Who Will Watch the Watchers?* edited by Didier Bigo, Emma McCluskey and Félix Tréguer, 203–30. London: Routledge.

Rogoff, Martin A. 1980. 'The International Legal Obligations of Signatories to an Unratified Treaty'. *Maine Law Review* 32, 263–99. https://mainelaw.maine.edu/faculty/wp-content/uploads/sites/4/rogoff-mlr-32.pdf.

Rose, Thomas. 2002. 'A Delicate Balance: Extradition, Sovereignty, and Individual Rights in the United States and Canada'. *Yale Journal of International Law* 27, no. 1: 193–215. https://openyls.law.yale.edu/bitstream/handle/20.500.13051/6441/11_27YaleJIntlL193_Winter2002_.pdf?sequence=2.

Ross, Jeffrey I. 2011. 'Moving Beyond Soering: U.S. Prison Conditions as an Argument against Extradition to the United States'. *International Criminal Justice Review* 21, no. 2: 156–68. https://doi.org/10.1177/1057567711408083.

Rossner, Meredith, Tait, David and McCurdy, Martha. 2021. 'Justice Reimagined: Challenges and Opportunities with Implementing Virtual Courts'. *Current Issues in Criminal Justice* 33, no. 1: 94–110. https://doi.org/10.1080/10345329.2020.1859968.

Rothe, Dawn L. and Mullins, Chrisopher W. 2010. 'The Death of State Sovereignty? An Empirical Exploration'. *International Journal of Comparative and Applied Criminal Justice* 34, no. 1: 79–96. https://doi.org/10.1080/01924036.2010.9678818.

Royce, Sylvia. 2009. 'International Prisoner Transfer'. *Federal Sentencing Reporter* 21, no. 3: 186–93. https://doi.org/10.1525/fsr.2009.21.3.186.

Sarmiento, Daniel. 2008. 'European Union: The European Arrest Warrant and the Quest for Constitutional Coherence'. *International Journal of Constitutional Law* 6, no. 1: 171–83. https://doi.org/10.1093/icon/mom040.

Segal, Murray D. 2019. 'Independent Review of the Extradition of Dr. Hassan Diab'. *Department of Justice Canada*. https://www.justice.gc.ca/eng/rp-pr/cj-jp/ext/01/review_ extradition_hassan_diab.pdf.

Semmelman, Jacques. 1999. 'The Rule of Non-Contradiction in International Extradition Proceedings: A Proposed Approach to the Admission of Exculpatory Evidence'. *Fordham International Law Journal* 23, no. 5: 1295–333. https://ir.lawnet. fordham.edu/ilj/vol23/iss5/2/.

Shea, Michael. 1992. 'Expanding Judicial Scrutiny of Human Rights in Extradition Cases after Soering'. *Yale Journal of International Law* 17, no. 1: 85–138. https://openyls. law.yale.edu/handle/20.500.13051/6266.

Shearer, Ivan A. 1966. 'Non-Extradition of Nationals: A Review and a Proposal'. *Adelaide Law Review* 2, no. 3: 273–309. http://www5.austlii.edu.au/au/journals/ AdelLawRw/1966/1.pdf.

Sheptycki, James. 2011. 'Transnational and Comparative Criminology Reconsidered'. In *Comparative Criminal Justice and Globalization*, edited by David Nelken, 145–61. Farnham: Routledge.

Sicalides, Barbara. 1989. 'Rico, CCE, and International Extradition'. *Temple Law Review* 62, no. 4: 1281–316. https://heinonline.org/HOL/LandingPage?handle=hein.journals/ temple62&div=63&id=&page=.

Stamatel, Janet P. 2009. 'Contributions of Cross-National Research to Criminology at the Beginning of the 21st Century'. In *Handbook on Crime and Deviance*, edited by Marvin D. Krohn, Alan J. Lizotte and Gina P. Hall, 3–22. New York: Springer. https://doi.org/10.1007/978-1-4419-0245-0_1.

Stuart, Riley. 2024. 'Julian Assange Granted Leave to Appeal Against Extradition to US'. *ABC News*, 20 May. https://www.abc.net.au/news/2024-05-20/julian-assange-court-london-leave-to-appeal-hearing/103864212.

Sullivan, David B. 1991. 'Abandoning the Rule of Non-Inquiry in International Extradition'. *Hastings International and Comparative Law Review* 15, no. 1: 111–33. https://repository. uclawsf.edu/hastings_international_comparative_law_review/vol15/iss1/5/.

United Nations. 1990. *Model Treaty on Extradition*. Vienna: United Nations. https://www. unodc.org/pdf/model_treaty_extradition.pdf.

United Nations Office on Drugs and Crime. 2012. *Manual on Mutual Legal Assistance and Extradition*. Vienna: United Nations. https://www.unodc.org/documents/organized-crime/Publications/Mutual_Legal_Assistance_Ebook_E.pdf.

Urbas, Gregor. 2012. 'Cybercrime, Jurisdiction and Extradition: The Extended Reach of Cross-Border Law Enforcement'. *Journal of Internet Law* 16, no. 1: 7–17. https:// openresearch-repository.anu.edu.au/handle/1885/62131.

US Attorney's Office, District of New Jersey. 2017. 'Canadian Man Sentenced to 14 Years in Prison for Role in Cocaine Distribution Scheme'. *Press Release*, 5 October.

https://www.justice.gov/usao-nj/pr/canadian-man-sentenced-14-years-prison-role-cocaine-distribution-scheme.

US Attorney's Office, Southern District of New York. 2019. 'Irish Man Who Helped Operate the "Silk Road" Website Sentenced in Manhattan Federal Court to Over Six Years in Prison'. *Press Release*, July 25. https://www.justice.gov/usao-sdny/pr/irish-man-who-helped-operate-silk-road-website-sentenced-manhattan-federal-court-over.

Valverde, Mariana. 2009. 'Jurisdiction and Scale: Legal "Technicalities" as Resources for Theory'. *Social & Legal Studies* 18, no. 2: 139–57. https://doi.org/10.1177/0964663909103622.

Van Cleave, Rachel A. 1999. 'The Role of United States Federal Courts in Extradition Matters: The Rule of Non-Inquiry, Preventive Detention and Comparative Legal Analysis'. *Temple International & Comparative Law Journal* 13, no. 1: 27–56. https://core.ac.uk/download/pdf/233110406.pdf.

Vladisavljevic, Anja. 2018. 'Croatian Court Denies Early Release to "Captain Dragan"'. *Balkan Insight*, 15 November. https://balkaninsight.com/2018/11/15/croatia-s-court-denied-early-release-of-former-serbian-paramilitary-commander-11-15-2018/.

———. 2019. 'Croatian Court Denies Early Release to "Captain Dragan" again'. *Balkan Insight*, 27 September. https://balkaninsight.com/2019/09/27/croatian-court-denies-early-release-to-captain-dragan-again/.

Vozzella, Laura. 2019. '"They Didn't Break Me": German Man Convicted of Va. Double Murder Freed after 33 Years'. *The Washington Post*, 17 December. https://www.washingtonpost.com/local/virginia-news/they-didnt-break-me-german-man-convicted-of-va-double-murder-freed-after-33-years/2019/12/17/d10409a2-20ea-11ea-a153-dce4b94e4249_story.html.

Warren, Ian and Palmer, Darren. 2015. *Global Criminology*. NSW: Thomson Reuters.

Williams, Sharon A. 1991. 'The Double Criminality Rule and Extradition: A Comparative Analysis'. *Nova Law Review* 15, no. 2: 581–623. https://digitalcommons.osgoode.yorku.ca/cgi/viewcontent.cgi?referer=&httpsredir=1&article=1454&context=scholarly_works.

———. 1992. 'Human Rights Safeguards and International Cooperation in Extradition: Striking the Balance'. *Criminal Law Forum* 3, no. 2: 191–224. https://doi.org/10.1007/BF01096199.

Wolitz, David 2013. 'Criminal Jurisdiction and the Nation-State: Toward Bounded Pluralism'. *Oregon Law Review* 91, no. 3: 725–81. https://scholarsbank.uoregon.edu/xmlui/bitstream/handle/1794/13593/Wolitz.pdf?sequence=1&isAllowed=y.

Wong, Ha K. 1998. 'The Extra in Extradition: The Impact of *State v. Pang* on Extraditee Standing and Implicit Waiver'. *Journal of Legislation* 24, no. 1: 111–24. https://scholarship.law.nd.edu/cgi/viewcontent.cgi?article=1202&context=jleg.

Working Group on Arbitrary Detention. 2015. 'Opinion No. 54/2015 Concerning Julian Assange (Sweden and the United Kingdom of Great Britain and Northern Ireland)'. *Human Rights Council*, 4 December. https://www.ohchr.org/en/statements/2016/02/working-group-arbitrary-detention-deems-deprivation-liberty-mr-julian-assange?LangID=E&NewsID=17012.

Zedner, Lucia. 2010. 'Security, the State, and the Citizen: The Changing Architecture of Crime Control'. *New Criminal Law Review: An International and Interdisciplinary Journal* 13, no. 2: 379–403. https://doi.org/10.1525/nclr.2010.13.2.379.

Zelinsky, Aaron S. J. 2009. '"Khouzam v. Chertoff": Torture, Removal, and the Rule of Noninquiry'. *Yale Law & Policy Review* 28, no.1: 233–43. https://www.jstor.org/stable/27871293.
Zumbansen, Peer. 2010. 'Transnational Legal Pluralism'. *Transnational Legal Theory* 1, no. 2: 141–89. https://doi.org/10.1080/20414005.2010.11424506.
———. 2012. 'Defining the Space of Transnational Law: Legal Theory, Global Governance, and Legal Pluralism'. *Transnational Law & Contemporary Problems* 21, no. 2: 305–35. https://digitalcommons.osgoode.yorku.ca/clpe/59/.

Domestic Legislation

Canadian Charter of Rights and Freedoms (Canadian Charter). 1982. Effective 17 April 1982.
Canada *Extradition Act*. 1999. Effective 17 June 1999.
Canada *Mutual Legal Assistance in Criminal Matters Act*. 1985. Effective 28 July 1988.
New Zealand *Bill of Rights Act*. 1990. Effective 28 August 1990.
New Zealand *Copyright Act*. 1994. 15 December 1994.
New Zealand *Crimes Act*. 1961. Effective 1 November 1961.
New Zealand *Extradition Act*. 1999. Effective 20 May 1999.
United Kingdom *Human Rights Act*. 1998. Effective 2 October 2000.
United States *Espionage Act*. 1917. Effective 15 June 1917.
United States *Federal Rules of Criminal Procedure*. 1944. Effective 26 December 1944.

International Agreements

Convention against Torture and Other Cruel, Unusual or Degrading Treatment or Punishment (CAT). 1984. Signed 10 December 1984, effective 26 June 1987.
Convention against Transnational Organized Crime. 2000. Signed 12 December 2000, effective 29 September 2003.
Convention on Cybercrime (Budapest Convention). 2001. Signed 23 November 2001, effective 1 July 2004.
Convention Relating to the Status of Refugees (Refugee Convention). 1951. Signed 28 July 1951, effective 22 April 1954.
European Convention on Human Rights (ECHR). 1950. Signed 4 November 1950, effective 3 September 1953.
International Covenant on Civil and Political Rights (ICCPR). 1966. Signed 16 December 1966, effective 23 March 1976.
Rome Statute of the International Criminal Court. 1998. Signed 17 July 1998, effective 1 July 2002.
Treaty on Extradition between Australia and the United States of America. 1976. Effective 4 August 1976.
Treaty on Extradition between the Government of Canada and the Government of the United States of America. 1976. Effective 22 March 1976.
Treaty on Extradition between New Zealand and the United States of America. 1970. Effective 8 December 1970.
Universal Declaration of Human Rights (UDHR). 1948. Effective 10 December 1948.

Cases

Assange's Application, Re (No. 2). 2018a. Westminster Magistrates' Court no. 1800196207.
Assange v Swedish Prosecution Authority. 2011. EWHC 2849 (Admin).
Assange v Swedish Prosecution Authority. 2012. UKSC 22.
Attorney-General v Davis. 2016. IEHC 497.
Bulaman v Canada. 2015. QCCA 1473.
Diab v France et al. 2014b. SCC 35889.
Dotcom v Attorney-General. 2012. NZHC 1494.
Dotcom et al. v United States of America. 2014. NZSC 24.
Einhorn v France. 2001. ECtHR application no. 71555/01.
France v Diab. 2010. ONSC 401.
France v Diab. 2011. ONSC 337.
France v Diab. 2014a. ONCA 374.
France v Tfaily. 2009. ONCA 5605.
France v Tfaily. 2010. ONCA 127.
Gallina v Fraser. 1960. US Dist. Crt. D. Conn. 278 F. 2d 77.
Gavrila v Canada (Justice). 2010. SCC 57.
Hilton v Kerry and Others. 2013b. US Dist. Crt. D. Mass. 151476.
Hilton v Kerry and Others. 2014. US App. 1st Cir. 11056.
India v Badesha. 2017. SCC 44.
In the Matter of the Extradition of Hilton. 2013a. US Dist. Crt. D. Mass. 63601.
In the Matter of the Extradition of Luna-Ruiz. 2014. US Dist. Crt. C.D. Cal. 36928.
In the Matter of the Extradition of Mujagic. 2013. US Dist. Crt. N.D.N.Y. 182801.
In the Matter of the Extradition of Nezirovic. 2013. US Dist. Crt. W.D. Va. 131873.
In re Normano. 1934. US Dist. Crt. D. Mass. 7 F. Supp. 329.
Martinez v United States of America. 2015. US App. 6th Cir. 11917.
McKinnon v United States of America. 2007. EWHC 762 (Admin).
McKinnon v United States of America and Another. 2008. UKHL 59.
Minister for Home Affairs of the Commonwealth v Zentai. 2012. HCA 28.
Németh v Canada (Justice). 2010. SCC 56.
Norris v United States of America. 2010. UKSC 9.
O'Connor v Adamas and Another. 2013. FCAFC 14.
Ortmann et al. v United States of America. 2018. NZCA 233.
Ortmann et al. v United States of America. 2020. NZSC 120.
Ortmann et al. v United States of America. 2021. NZCA 310.
Perez v Mims (Warden). 2016b. US Dist. Crt. E.D. Cal. 77406.
Perez v Mims (Warden). 2017a. US Dist. Crt. E.D. Cal. 11255.
Perez v Mims (Warden). 2017b. US Dist. Crt. E.D. Cal. 33406.
Republic of Croatia v Snedden. 2010. HCA 14.
Romania v Savu. 2008. QCCS 5079.
R v Assange. 2019a. Southwark Crown Court.
R v Diab. 2009. Sup. Cr. J. no. 12838.
R v Ortmann and van der Kolk. 2023. NZHC 1504.
Savu v Canada (Minister of Justice). 2013a. QCCA 554.
Savu v Canada (Minister of Justice). 2013b. QCCA 699.
Savu v Minister of Justice of Canada. 2013c. SCC 35316.
Snedden v Minister for Justice. 2013. FCA 1202.

Snedden v Minister for Justice and Another. 2014. FCAFC 156.

Snedden v Republic of Croatia. 2007. FCA 1902.

Snedden v Republic of Croatia. 2009a. FCA 30.

Snedden v Republic of Croatia. 2009b. FCAFC 111.

Söering v United Kingdom. 1989. ECtHR application no. 14038/88.

Suarez v Canada. 2014. QCCA 281.

Swedish Judicial Authority v Assange. 2010. EWHC 3473 (Admin).

Trabelsi v Belgium. 2014. ECtHR application no. 140/10.

Tsvetnenko v United States of America. 2019. FCAFC 74.

United States of America v Adam. 2014. BCCA 136.

United States of America v Assange. 2018b. US Dist. Crt. E.D. Va. 1:18cr.

United States of America v Assange. 2019b. US Dist. Crt. E.D. Va. 1:18-cr-111.

United States of America v Assange. 2020. US Dist. Crt. E.D. Va. 1:18-cr-111.

United States of America v Assange. 2021a. Westminster Magistrates' Court.

United States of America v Assange. 2021b. EWHC 2528 (Admin).

United States of America v Assange. 2021c. EWHC 3313 (Admin).

United States of America v Burns. 2001. SCC 7.

United States of America v Churuk. 2013. ONCA 330.

United States of America v Doak. 2013. BCSC 224.

United States of America v Giese. 2015. EWHC 3658 (Admin).

United States of America v Igwe. 2014. QCCS 6859.

United States of America v Le. 2014. ONSC 4823.

United States of America v McKinnon. 2002a. US Dist. Crt. D.N.J.

United States of America v McKinnon. 2002b. US Dist. Crt. E.D. Va.

United States of America v Perez. 2016a. US Dist. Crt. E.D. Cal. 31897.

United States of America v Talashkova. 2014. ONCA 74.

United States of America v Viscomi. 2015. ONCA 484.

Vasiljkovic v Commonwealth of Australia. 2006a. HCA 40.

Vasiljkovic v Minister for Justice and Customs and Others. 2006b. FCA 1346.

Vasiljkovic v O'Connor. 2010. FCA 1246.

Vasiljkovic v O'Connor (No 2). 2011. FCAFC 125.

INDEX

Milton Keynes UK
Ingram Content Group UK Ltd.
UKHW041126281024
450262UK00002B/92